**AUTHENTIC TRANSCRIPTIONS
WITH NOTES AND TABLATURE**

ROBERT JOHNSON

Transcribed by
SCOTT AINSLIE and
DAVE WHITEHILL

M000168536

ACKNOWLEDGEMENTS

Our own knowledge depends on the knowledge of those who have gone before. Some of those people for this book are: Stephen Calt, David Evans, Stephen LaVere, Mack McCormick, Gayle Dean Wardlow

Cover Photo: (computer enhanced) Studio Portrait, circa 1935
© Stephen C. LaVere 1989

**HAL•LEONARD™
CORPORATION**
7777 W. BLUEMOUND RD. P.O. BOX 13819 MILWAUKEE, WI 53213

ISBN 0-7935-1093-7

ROBERT JOHNSON

We'd be on the road for days and days, no money and sometimes not much food, let alone a decent place to spend the night, playing on dusty streets or inside dirty places of the sort you played in those times, and as I'd catch my breath and see myself looking like a <u>dog</u>, there'd be Robert all clean as can be looking like he just stepping out of church!"

—Johnny Shines

Robert Johnson was just a mercurial, mysterious presence laid down in the grooves of old acetate 78's. To whites, a polite, shy colored boy; to his audience and fellow Delta musicians, a shockingly talented, alternately pensive and reckless young bluesman who pestered and then surpassed his teachers. Much more is known about him today than when I began transcribing his music, yet most of what you need to know lies etched in the grooves of 50 year old acetate discs, and if you've heard them, etched in your memory, as well.

Eric Clapton refers to Robert Johnson as "the most important blues musician who ever lived." Keith Richards said, when he first heard Johnson's recordings "suddenly he raised the ante, suddenly you just had to aim that much higher." Ry Cooder, Taj Mahal, Johnny Winter, John Hammond, Rory Block, David

Studio Portrait, circa 1935

© Stephen C. LaVere 1989

Bromberg – many of today's most prominent and inspired blues performers track an important part of what they know about music to these 29 songs recorded by a musician who was dead before he was 28.

With the release of his entire recorded output by Columbia-CBS Records and the imminent publication of much of the fieldwork that has been done by two especially important researchers, Mack McCormick and Stephen LaVere – some might hope that the mystery of Robert Johnson could be put to rest, that a healing might take place to unite the sound of this man with our impression of his life. To some extent this may be possible: it is certainly wonderful to have the recordings and information available at last. But we are left with a large gap between how, where and when Johnson lived – and why he did what he did in two temporary recording studios in Texas in the fall of 1936 and summer of '37. All the information we could ever hope to have about Robert Johnson will ultimately fall short of explaining his talent – the very part of his life we would most like to hear explained.

The closest Dave Whitehill and I have come to answering this is tied up in these transcriptions: in the act of putting our guitars and our hands parallel to his and allowing them to resonate with his effort and his music. This book is our way of recommending the experience to you. It is the only remotely successful way I know to close the half-century gap that separates us from Robert Johnson. If you will know the man get in tune, put your fingers where his fingers were, and commit yourself to the sound the way he did.

Music at its best has a mystical, transforming power. After a half century, there is no doubt that Johnson's spectacularly raw and sophisticated blues are some of the best music around. In some cases, the closer I have examined music, the less interesting it has appeared – it doesn't hold up to concentrated attention. This has not been true with Johnson's guitar parts. They are even richer for me now than they were before I tackled the transcriptions. I hope the same will be true for you.

—Scott Ainslie
Thanksgiving, 1991
Durham, North Carolina

CONTENTS

THE BIOGRAPHY

Robert Leroy Johnson came into this world on May 8, 1911, near the town of Hazelhurst, Mississippi. Even before he got here, there was trouble waiting for him.

In 1889, Robert's mother, Julia Ann Major, the daughter of parents who were born into slavery in Mississippi, married Charles Dodds. Also born of former slaves (but in North Carolina), Dodds was an enterprising carpenter and wicker furniture maker. By the early 1900's, they owned their own land and house, and had a large family – by any standard, especially in the black community, they were doing quite well. But in 1909, things took a bad turn. Dodds apparently injured a member of a prominent white family (the Marchetti brothers) in a fight and had to flee Hazelhurst with a lynch mob in close pursuit.

Left behind with ten children, Julia managed to hang onto the house and land. Over the next couple of years she sent the children – one by one – up to Memphis to stay with their father, who was living under the name of Charles Spencer. Julia remained behind with her two daughters, Carrie and Bessie. During their separation, Charles took a mistress in Memphis and had two children by her. In his absence, Julia took up with Noah Johnson, an itinerant sharecropper. It was with him that she conceived and bore a boy, whom she named Robert Leroy.

Within two years, Julia had been evicted from her property (with a little help from the Marchetti family), ostensibly for non-payment of taxes, and

LaVere, Carrie related that her father, Charlie, welcomed the woman back but she didn't stay long.

By around 1914, the whole family was together in Memphis: Charlie Spencer, Julia and their ten children, Spencer's mistress and their two children, and Robert. While the two women apparently got along, Julia struck out on her own, leaving the children in Memphis. Shortly afterward, the family heard that Julia had died and grieved for her loss for over a year.

Around 1916, Carrie recognized Julia walking near Beale and Front Streets. "That's mama," she exclaimed. She had returned to Memphis to ask Charlie's permission to remarry. Julia was living near Robinsonville with Willie 'Dusty' Willis, a hard-working farm hand. Spencer was beginning to have a problem disciplining the strong-willed boy, so it was agreed that Robert, then 4 or 5, would return to the Delta to live with Julia and 'Dusty'. It was in Commerce – a small sharecropping settlement of about 150 near Robinsonville, about forty miles south of Memphis – that Robert grew up.

While 'Dusty' Willis was out working in the fields around Commerce, his stepson Robert took up 'Jew's' harp and harmonica, trading songs and verses with friends. By all accounts, Robert was thoroughly uninterested in farm work and a lot of friction developed between Robert and his stepfather. Around 1927, Robert got his first guitar.

In 1929, at the age of 18, Robert fell in love with and married Virginia Travis. They moved in with his

Wisconsin, Son was a powerful performer. Half bluesman and half preacher, his passionate performances impressed the young musician. Robert, still relatively new to the guitar, would sit at the feet of Willie Brown, Son House (and perhaps occasionally Charley Patton) studying their techniques and arrangements; absorbing their styles in the raucous atmosphere of the juke joints. He often made a nuisance of himself – commandeering one of their guitars when they were on break and running the patrons out of the joint with his inexperienced playing. Son House recalled scolding him more than a few times, and encouraged the young musician to stick with the harmonica. Robert didn't pay him much mind.

Sneaking out to the joints (his stepfather, in particular, was against it), Robert began to acquire some style and playing experience of his own. Elizabeth Moore, a local sharecropper, recalled seeing Robert play (with Willie Brown backing him up!) in a juke just north of Robinsonville. In late 1930, Elizabeth's husband, Willie Moore – a former playing partner of Charley Patton and Willie Brown – chanced upon Robert playing in front of a Robinsonville grocery and joined him in a jam. She reported that they were both picked up and spent several hours in the local jail for singing about the sheriff!

Feeling his oats as a performer and wondering about his roots and his own father (having had fairly rocky relationships with two stepfathers), Robert went back to Hazelhurst, the only clue he had to his past, and began searching for his father.

It was there, in May of 1931, that Robert married Calletta Craft ("Callie") at the Copiah County Courthouse. Callie was a generous, affectionate woman who had been married twice before and had three children. Although Robert insisted that their marriage be kept a secret, Callie adored Robert and kept him in food and shelter – often fixing him breakfast in bed. Meanwhile, Robert met Ike Zinnerman, a veteran guitarist from Alabama, and apprenticed himself to the older musician. Robert would often spend entire weekends playing with Zinnerman, a fine unrecorded guitarist who was fluent in East Coast and Delta styles who claimed to have learned how to play by sitting in a graveyard on tombstones at night. With Callie, Robert established a pattern that he was to follow in the coming years everywhere he went. Seeking out older, often less attractive women, he would exchange his attentions for their kindness and the refuge they offered him: using the time their labor gave him to advance his skills as a musician. Mack McCormick found at least half a dozen women who had relationships of this nature with Robert – most of them lasting two to three weeks. The most durable of these, however, were with Willie Mae Cross (a cousin of David 'Honeyboy' Edwards) in Tunica, Mississippi, and Estella Coleman (Robert 'Jr.' Lockwood's mother) in Helena. Callie was not one of them. Robert deserted her in the mid-'30s. She had a nervous breakdown and died several years later – never having seen Robert again.

In late 1930 Elizabeth's husband, Willie Moore – a former playing partner of Charlie Patton and Willie Brown – chanced upon Robert playing in front of a Robinsonville Grocery and joined him in a jam. She reported that they were both picked up and spent several hours in the local jail for singing about the sheriff!

signed on with a migrant labor company in the Delta. Robert's first years were spent moving from plantation to plantation. Carrie, his eight year old half-sister, would care for him while Julia picked and chopped cotton. Over the next few years, Julia struggled to unite the family, but according to researcher Mack McCormick, "Robert was the stumbling block. This outside child was very much resented by Charlie (Dodds) Spencer." In a conversation with Stephen

half-sister Bessie and her husband. In August, Virginia became pregnant. Robert was an attentive husband and a proud, expectant father, staying close to home and working the fields, more a fieldhand than a musician. However, on April 10, 1930, both Virginia and the baby died in labor. She was 16 years old.

Within a few months, as if to fill the hole in Robert's life, Son House moved to Robinsonville. Having just recorded with Willie Brown in Grafton,

FAR LEFT: Don Law
LEFT: Robert Johnson's mother,
Julia Ann Majors, c. 1915
ABOVE: Robert's half sister Carrie
Thompson, outside Washington
D.C., June 22, 1974

Traveling extensively through the Delta and up into Tennessee, Robert had, in addition to his sexual refuges (and due to his complicated family history), half-brothers and half-sisters, cousins and half-cousins, aunts and uncles who could take him in on short notice and make him feel at home.

In the fall of 1936, Johnson went to the one man known throughout the Delta for his influence with the record companies – the man responsible for recording Charley Patton, Son House, Skip James, the Mississippi Sheiks, Tommy Johnson, and practically every other Delta musician of note: H.C. Speir.

Speir owned a music store in Jackson, Mississippi and initially got involved with scouting talent in order to earn additional income. Speir was an admirer of many different styles of music, but his taste in blues seems to have been impeccable.

Robert may have auditioned with "Kind Hearted Woman." Speir remembered Johnson as a young blues musician – not overwhelming, but worth passing along to Ernie Oertle, the American Record Company's regional representative for Louisiana and Mississippi. (Remember that Speir had worked with some of the very finest blues musicians ever to be recorded. Robert seemed like a good prospect to him.) Speir often cut test records in the store, and Robert may have made one that afternoon. (His half-sister Carrie recalls Robert giving her a record like that, which she played until she wore it out and threw away.)

Oertle sought out Robert, heard him play, and offered to take him to San Antonio to record. According to Mack McCormick, Robert was elated and rushed over to share the news with Carrie.

Oertle and Johnson traveled together to San Antonio, arriving for Johnson's first day of recording on November 23, 1936. ARC had set up a makeshift recording studio in the downtown area (long thought to be in the Gunter Hotel, although the exact location has been called into question in recent years and it may have taken place at a local radio station's studio). Don Law, ARC's Regional Sales Branch Manager, was in charge of the sessions – which were apparently pretty hectic affairs. All the regional talent thought to be worth recording converged on one location. Musicians of all kinds: Mexican, hillbilly, gospel, and blues could be found crowded in the lobby and hallways waiting for their turn in front of the microphone.

According to a report in the San Antonio Light on November 23rd, "(the) Brunswick (ARC's sister company) recording crew here figures it set a record when it got under the wire with 105 recordings made in the first three days of its San Antonio set up." While impressive, this report is most likely an exaggeration since records from the sessions show fewer recordings per day than were cited in the article. A little bravado certainly wouldn't hurt the excitement of having the record company in town, or future sales, for that matter.

As widely reported, Don Law recalled Robert as a shy musician of perhaps only 18 or 19. According to Law's son, Don Law, Jr., both his parents had vivid memories of Johnson. His mother, Hazel Maxfield Law, a concert pianist, remarked about Johnson's hands which with their long graceful fingers showed excellent proportions for an instrumentalist. She also remembered that when they were walking on the street with Robert and trying to carry on a conversation with him, Johnson would keep falling in a few steps behind them. They would encourage him to step up and walk with them, which he would do for a few steps, only to fall in quietly behind them again. As Don Law, Jr. tells it, it was awkward for all of them.

Don Law, Sr. was British and apparently quite an easy-going, relaxed sort of man. As a Briton, he was naturally not raised or vested in the culture of the White or Black south. Johnson's reticence about walking and conversing with them must have seemed foreign to Law and he put it down in his mind to shyness. But Robert's behavior in the mid 1930s, in the white business districts of downtown San Antonio and Dallas with a well-dressed white couple must have differed wildly from his behavior on his own turf in the joints, alleyways and street corners of the Delta. His recorded performances alone completely contradict this impression – exposing the passion and magnetism of the 25 year old musician.

Law also recalled that Robert was too nervous and shy to sit down and play a tune for some of the Mexican musicians. According to Law, Johnson had to turn away and face the wall before he could compose himself enough to play – and then he played without ever facing his audience. That this episode was rooted in shyness or inexperience again seems mistaken. More than likely, Robert was reluctant to show his technique to other practiced, professional musicians. He was acutely aware that he was doing something new with the guitar – synthesizing and surpassing the Delta guitar masters of the previous generation – and he jealously guarded his techniques. This was how he made his living!

By all accounts, Robert had one of the quickest ears in the Delta. According to Johnny Shines, he could keep up a conversation with you while listening to some new piece on the radio and play it for you note for note hours or even days later. This facility shows up in his guitar parts which combine influences from Lonnie Johnson, Son House, Charley Patton, Skip James, Tommy Johnson and others – one moment playing thick rhythmic chords, then punctuating it with single string slides sharp and clean enough to draw blood. His accompaniments either portray or throw into bold relief the lyrics and meaning of the songs.

Few people recall hearing Robert practice or work up a new piece. When he picked up the guitar with people around, it was to work, to perform, to impress. Many of the women Mack McCormick interviewed remembered how they would wake up in the middle of the night to find Robert noiselessly fingering the guitar strings in the faint light of the window. As soon as he realized they were awake he would stop. Robert seemed almost consciously involved in creating the myth his work would later inspire.

On his first day in the studio, Monday, November 23, 1936, Robert recorded eight different tunes:

"Kindhearted Woman Blues" (#SA-2580-1,2)
"I Believe I'll Dust My Broom" (#SA-2581-1,2)
"Sweet Home Chicago" (#SA-2582-1,2)
"Ramblin' On My Mind" (#SA-2583-1,2)
"When You Got A Good Friend" (#SA-2584-1,2)
"Come On In My Kitchen" (#SA-2585-1,2)
"Terraplane Blues" (#SA-2586-1,2)
"Phonograph Blues" (#SA-2586-1,2)

By all accounts, Robert had one of the quickest ears in the Delta. According to Johnny Shines, he could keep up a conversation with you while listening to some new piece on the Radio and play it for you note-for-note hours or even days later.

(Matrix numbers: SA = location; four digit title sequence number; -1,2 = surviving takes in order of producer's preference.)

Many takes were often made of each number, of which the session's producer would select two. One was intended to be a 'safety' – as close in feel and technique as possible to the preferred performance. Not all the takes survived. Recorded on wax masters, they were sometimes damaged in transit when shipped back to New York. They could literally melt if the temperatures got too high. (Notes on the individual songs introduce the transcriptions.)

Robert didn't record again until Thursday, November 26th. The delay seems unwarranted until we consider Don Law's apocryphal story about Robert's first night in the 'big city'. Law recounted the story to Frank Driggs of Columbia records, years after the fact. Driggs wrote:

"...Don Law considered himself responsible for Johnson, found him a room in a boarding house and told him to get some sleep so he would be ready to begin recording at ten the following morning. Law then joined his wife and some friends for dinner at the Gunter Hotel. He had scarcely begun dinner when he was summoned to the phone. A policeman was calling from the city jail. Johnson had been picked up on a vagrancy charge. Law rushed down to the jail, found Johnson beaten up, his guitar smashed; the cops had not only picked him up but had worked him over. With some difficulty, Law managed to get Johnson freed in his custody, whisked him back to the boarding house, gave him forty-five cents for breakfast, and told him to stay in the house and not to go out for the rest of the evening. Law returned to the hotel, only to be called to the phone again. This time it was Johnson. Fearing the worst, Law asked, 'What's the matter now?' Johnson replied, 'I'm lonesome.' Puzzled, Law said, 'You're lonesome? What do you mean, you're lonesome?' Johnson replied, 'I'm

RIGHT: Ike Zinnerman, Robert Johnson's mentor and guitar teacher

lonesome and there's a lady here. She wants fifty cents and I lacks a nickel...'

Apparently Johnson, having nothing to do, went into a joint somewhere to play for change and the place got raided. If this story is essentially correct, it may account for the delay.

In any event, Johnson was back in the studio on Thursday, November 26th for two takes of:
"32-20 Blues" (#SA-2616-1,2)

Some of Robert's most powerful and memorable recordings came the following day, Friday, November 27th. After warming up with a couple of 'hokum' blues pieces, Johnson tuned up into open A and bared his soul with several of his slide guitar masterpieces. In this last session in San Antonio he recorded:
"They're Red Hot" (#SA-2627-1,2)
"Dead Shrimp Blues" (#SA-2628-1,2)
"Cross Road Blues" (#SA-2629-1,2)
"Walking Blues" (#SA-2630-1,2)
"Last Fair Deal Gone Down" (#SA-2631-1,2)
"Preaching Blues" (#SA-2632-1,2)
"If I Had Possession Over Judgement Day"
 (#SA-2633-1,2)

Once his music was on the jukeboxes, Robert was a recording star. The jukebox had become an important source of material for musicians all over the Delta – a mechanical extension of the oral culture that musicians depended on to keep up with current trends. Robert traveled extensively: Memphis, St. Louis, Decatur, Chicago, Detroit, New York City, Buffalo, even Ontario, Canada. He visited his extended family in the Delta. Even his father, Noah Johnson, is said to have crossed paths with him during this period.

"We heard a couple of his pieces come out on records," Son House recalled. "Believe the first one I

that served as the regional distribution point for Brunswick Records. In an open warehouse area that they had isolated with baffles, he cut three masters:
"Stones In My Passway" (#DAL-377-1,2,3)
"I'm A Steady Rollin' Man" (#DAL-378-1,2,3)
"From Four Till Late" (#DAL-379-1,2)

On the next day, Sunday the 20th, Robert returned to the makeshift studio to make what were to be his final ten recordings. Eerily, as if he could foresee what was to come, Robert began the session with one of his most chilling pieces. It was an exhausting, impressive day of recording:
"Hellhound On My Trail" (#DAL-394-1,2)
"Little Queen Of Spades" (#DAL-395-1,2)
"Malted Milk" (#DAL-396-1,2)
"Drunken Hearted Man" (#DAL-397-1,2)
"Me And The Devil Blues" (#DAL-398-1,2)
"Stop Breakin' Down Blues" (#DAL-399-1,2)
"Traveling Riverside Blues" (#DAL-400-1,2)
"Honeymoon Blues" (#DAL-401-1,2)
"Love In Vain" (#DAL-402-1,2,3,4)
"Milkcow's Calf Blues" (#DAL-403-1,2,3)

When Robert Johnson walked out into the Dallas streets that evening – possibly exhausted, elated – he had guaranteed his place in music history. With these twenty-nine recordings, made in five sessions just seven months apart, Robert was to change the course of the Delta's musical history, and with it the history of rock 'n' roll.

Johnson is reported to have headed down into Texas' cotton country after the sessions. Johnny Shines remembers hooking up with him in Red Water, Texas and playing around the area until the cold weather set in. They separated and Shines went on to his mother's place in Arkansas. Robert

Photo by ROBERT BARCLAY

"I'd hung around with Robert about two years off and on. The last time me and him was together we was coming out of Memphis. I was going my way to Robinsonville, and he was on his way to Greenwood..."
–Howlin' Wolf

"So he left and went out there from Greenwood, Mississippi. The next word we heard was from his mother, who told us he was dead."
–Son House

Greenwood, Mississippi was to be Robert's undoing. The circumstances of Robert's death, as they circulated around the Delta from musician to musician, perhaps tell us more about the dangers awaiting the traveling musician than anything else. Some said he'd been poisoned, some said stabbed, some said both. It was reported that he crawled on his hands and knees and barked like a dog before he died – as if he really had learned to play from the devil at the crossroads, and his note had come due.

After years of painstaking, numbing research, Gayle Dean Wardlow and Mack McCormick each independently located Robert's death certificate in the state capital (Jackson, MS), thirty years after his death. Using it as a starting point, McCormick managed, after hundreds of fruitless interviews, to find witnesses to the murder and to piece together the circumstances of Robert's death. The account McCormick has put together agrees substantially with the memory of David 'Honeyboy' Edwards, who had been playing with Robert in the Greenwood area in the weeks before Johnson's death. On Robert's last weekend, they were booked to play at a dance in Three Forks, about 15 miles out from Greenwood. That was Friday, August 12th and Saturday, August 13th, 1938.

"How I got it, this fellow said Robert was messing around with his wife or something like that. So Robert came back to Greenwood and went back the next Saturday night out there. So he gave some of his friends some whiskey to give Robert to

"I'd hung around with Robert about two years off and on. The last time me and him was together we was coming out of Memphis. I was going my way to Robinsonville and he was on his way to Greenwood..." – Howlin' Wolf

heard was 'Terraplane Blues'. Jesus, it was good! We all admired it. Said, 'That boy is really going places'."

Robert was called back to Texas seven months later (this time to Dallas) to record again for ARC. His "Terraplane Blues" had been a modest hit in the race record market, selling perhaps as many as 4 to 5,000 copies, and the company was anxious to follow it up with other material.

On Saturday, June 19, 1937, Johnson walked up to the third floor of the office building

just went on. He spent some time in Memphis, and in Helena at Estella Coleman's. His recordings continued to be released. He was playing jukes and rent parties, country frolics and streetcorners – sometimes with Shines and sometimes without.

"Then Robert went over into Mississippi. I didn't like Mississippi, so I didn't go with him, and I never saw Robert again."

–Johnny Shines

Photo © by TOM COPI

ABOVE: Son House at 1969 Ann
Arbor Blues Festival
BELOW: David "Honeyboy"
Edwards at the 1988 Chicago
Blues Festival
OPPOSITE PAGE: Robert Junior
Lockwood at the 1991 Chicago
Blues Festival.
LEFT: Johnny Shines at the 1991
Chicago Blues Festival.

Photo by ROBERT BARCLAY

Photo by ROBERT BARCLAY

drink – I was lucky I didn't drink none of the whiskey, but I don't guess they was trying to give it to me. His friend give it to Robert – you see, he give it to him to drink because he had it in for Robert and his wife. But he still keep him to play for him! I think this fellow was named Ralph.

"About 1:00 Robert taken sick when he was playing. All the people just came out the city said they wanted him to play, 'cause they was drinking and all them having a good time, and they was begging him to play, and he played sick. And they said he told the public, he said, 'Well, I'm sick, y'all see, but I'm playing, but I'm still sick. I'm not able to play.' About 2:00 he got so sick they had to bring him back to town…"

–David 'Honeyboy' Edwards

In the account recently published with the Columbia-CBS release of Johnson's complete recordings, researcher Stephen LaVere adds some interesting details to the story. Edwards was not able to get to the joint until around 10:30 that evening, but Sonny Boy Williamson II was there and joined Johnson for the gig. With these two lions of Delta blues harmonica and guitar, one can imagine the excitement generated in the club. According to Sonny Boy, (who may have been more fond of a good story than concerned with factual details)

Robert became quite obvious in his display of affection for a woman at the joint. She was, indeed, the wife of their employer for the evening. Sonny Boy quickly recognized the stony faces and who was talking to whom and sized up the situation. When a half-pint of whiskey with a broken seal came around to Robert, the older and wiser Sonny Boy knocked it out of his hand, just as he was about to take a drink. It broke on the ground. "Man, don't never take a drink from an open bottle. You don't know what could be in it." Sonny Boy said. Angered, Robert said, "Man, don't never knock a bottle of whiskey outta my hand."

When a second bottle came around with a broken seal, Sonny Boy could only stand and

"So he left and went out there from Greenwood, Mississippi. The next word we heard was from his Mother, who told us he was dead."

— Son House

RIGHT: *Abbay & Leatherman Plantation Commissary on the plantation where Robert grew up, 1974.* CENTER: *Robert Johnson's Death Certificate.* FAR RIGHT: *Robert Johnson's Grave, Mt. Zion Church. South of Morgan City, MS, June 26, 1991.*

Photo STEPHEN C. LAVERE © 1974

Photo LAURI LAWSON © 1991

CERTIFIED COPY OF RECORD OF DEATH

I, Alton B. Cobb, M.D., State Registrar of Vital Statistics, hereby certify this to be a true and correct copy of the death record of the person named therein, the original being on file in this office.

Given at Jackson, Mississippi, over my signature and under the official seal of my office, this the 18th day of July, 1973.

Alton B. Cobb, M.D., State Registrar

Paul Burnell Hawkins
Paul Burnell Hawkins, Deputy State Registrar

watch. (One salient problem with this account is that Mississippi was a dry state in the 1930's and bootleg whiskey was *very* rarely, if ever, sold in sealed bottles – still, it is a great story.)

At some point after the poisoning, 'Honeyboy' Edwards showed up. By the time 'Honeyboy' got there, Robert was already feeling pretty bad. Before long, he couldn't sing. Then he couldn't play. He went outside and was ill. Strong enough to withstand the poisoning, Robert survived the night. For several days, he lay trying to recuperate at a friend's home, but, weakened by the poisoning, he apparently contracted pneumonia, for which there was no cure before 1946. He passed away that Tuesday, August 16th, 1938.

According to one account, his body was buried by his family in a coffin supplied by the county in the cemetery of Zion Church. Recently, other accounts have surfaced placing his gravesite in question again. But in any event, Robert Johnson – referred to in Melody Maker's July, 1937 issue as "Hot Spring's recording star" – was dead at the age of twenty-seven.

ROBERT JOHNSON had six recordings in circulation at the time of his death. John Hammond

(Sr.) was searching for him for his first "From Spirituals to Swing" concert which was held December 23rd, 1938 at Carnegie Hall. Notified of Johnson's death just a week before the concert, Hammond wrote a eulogy of sorts, hired Big Bill Broonzy to take Robert's place in the bill, and played two of Robert's recordings from the stage: "Walkin' Blues" and "Preachin' Blues."

With the exception of a handful of blues researchers and Delta musicians, Johnson's relative obscurity persisted until 1962 when Columbia Records issued sixteen of Robert's recordings on **Robert Johnson: King of the Delta Blues Singers**. Volume II was released in 1971. With these recordings the torch was passed to a new generation of musicians – the likes of the Rolling Stones and Eric Clapton. His music continues to be cited as a seminal influence by many of today's heavy metal guitarists, and for all of today's

electric and acoustic slide guitarists.

The strength of Johnson's work in the studio, combined with the mysterious circumstances, that until recently have shrouded his death, have inspired numerous articles, books and films. In addition to **Crossroads**, which was only nominally about Johnson – Alan Greenberg's screenplay, *Love in Vain*, is heading into production at Warner Brothers as this book goes to press. And this won't be the end of it. With the availability of so much new information about Johnson's life, and of all his recordings – we are finally free to wonder about the central core of Robert's genius and talent. It is there our attention will rest in the years to come.

–Scott Ainslie
Durham, North Carolina

Hazlehurst sign. Hazlehurst, Mississippi, April 1974

Photo STEPHEN C. LAVERE ©

ON THE TRANSCRIPTIONS

In the 1930's, it was standard practice to make duplicate takes of each piece an artist recorded, to serve as a safety and to provide record companies with at least two options when deciding whether or not to release a given tune. With Columbia's recent release of **Robert Johnson: The Complete Recordings**, choices had to be made on which versions of the tunes would be selected for transcription. The takes chosen are identified by their original take numbers (assigned to them during their recording in 1936 and 1937) and their selection was based on the authority of the performances. These selections coincide with earlier releases included in Columbia's **Robert Johnson: King of the Delta Blues Singers** (1962) and **Volume II** (1971). Where distinctive additional lyrics have come to light with the release of Johnson's outtakes, those lyrics have been included here.

Johnson's slide pieces (all in open tunings) have had a remarkable impact on guitarists. The popularity of his material and his clean, forceful articulation of slide notes continues to fascinate and inspire new generations of players. Contemporary slide performance practice favors open G-tuning (low to high: D-G-D-G-B-D) and D-tuning (D-A-D-F♯-A-D). There has been a tendency to assume Johnson must have used these tunings, capoing up to create the absolute pitch of the recordings. However, a careful review of Johnson's pieces and the actual logistics of slide technique argue against these assumptions. With many of Johnson's original recordings in the keys of B and F♯, in G or D-tuning he would have had to place his capo on the fourth fret. This would make the octave of the open string four frets above the neck-body joint on the 12-fret guitar neck that was standard in the '30s, and required impossibly awkward left-hand histrionics. Therefore, it is likely that Johnson used open A-tuning (E-A-E-A-C♯-E) and open E-tuning (E-B-E-G♯-B-E), which are parallel to open G and D-tunings, respectively. The fingerings are identical in open A and open G-tuning – while the absolute pitches will be simply a whole step higher or lower (the same is true for open E and open D-tuning). The transcriptions here are presented in open A and E-tunings and instructions are included in the introductions to each transcription on capoing to match pitches with the recordings. Should you wish to attempt to play these pieces in G or D-tuning, you will have to adjust the capo up a whole tone (two frets) to compensate for the lower tuning.

One of the thorniest problems for any transcriber is how to notate the idiosyncratic rhythmic variations in Johnson's music. The apparently erratic length of Johnson's measures reflects his use of rhythm as a distinct, expressive element in his performances. In the same way western music varies harmony and melody for expressive effect, Johnson stalls and startles the listener with added or dropped beats.

Rhythm in popular ensemble music is used as a means of keeping the band together – a sort of straitjacket that defies individual additions or subtractions. But the solo performer has unlimited rhythmic flexibility and Johnson exploits this freedom at every opportunity. While performers in other solo musical traditions, such as the mountain fiddling of West Virginia and a cappella ballad singing of Ireland and the Appalachians, routinely employ irregular measures with added or dropped beats, the use and importance of the expressive rhythmic variation in African musical traditions must also be seen as playing an important role in Johnson's choices as a performer.

Johnson's music lies right on the border between original and traditional music, and the inevitable (and often apparently arbitrary) decisions about where to put the barline need to be informed by the traditions which influenced Johnson's work. The genealogy of blues includes communal worksongs and individual field hollers, humorous songs and spirituals. The free melismatic melodic ornament of the field holler; the heartfelt delivery of the gospel singer; the 'camp' vocal quality of the humorous singer/storyteller and the rhythmic structure of the worksong all come to bear on Johnson's performance style. (A more detailed discussion of worksong rhythms can be found in the introductory notes for "Cross Road Blues" and "Walking Blues," where these rhythmic elements have influenced rhythmic variation quite directly.)

In general, you should note that Johnson adds and drops beats without altering the emphasis found in the normal 4/4 measure: a 3/4 measure is never played like a waltz, nor is a 5/4 measure ever broken into 3-2 grouping. The added beat is just that, and not generally cause for a re-interpretation of the stresses within the measure. Where possible I have grouped beats to indicate the downbeats in the measure. Occasionally this has required odd-looking measures of 1/4. Added and dropped beats can be assumed to be at the end of measures, rather than at the beginning due to this emphasis on the downbeat in the successive measure.

The last note about rhythmic notation involves the editorial choice to employ 4/4 rather than 12/8 as the basic meter for these transcriptions. While the rhythmic emphasis in Delta blues almost always warrants measures of 12/8 and triple meters within the beat, we believe that in 12/8 measures it is often difficult to see the 4/4 feel of the music, and that the note values are visually misleading to all but the most experienced readers. Accordingly, we have chosen to notate triplets with the standard indication.

While the 12/8, triplet oriented notation is generally most accurate, Johnson's exceptions (where true sixteenth and eighth notes appear) and the cleaner visual representations of the 4/4 feel of the music have controlled our decision. Since this music will be almost impossible to play if the ear does not have a firm grasp on the material, these transcriptions will be most useful when paired with Johnson's recordings.

Johnson's right-hand plucking technique is often quite complicated. He often uses his thumb to strike notes on the treble strings of the guitar. Many of us are used to keeping the thumb on the bass strings and the fingers on the treble strings. In the transcriptions, we have indicated notes played with the thumb with the note-stems going down and finger-articulated notes with the note-stems going up. While great care has been taken to notate Johnson's right-hand mechanics, the notations here are certainly open to alternate interpretations. In many cases, the cleanness and force of Johnson's treble-string slides and the direction of his strumming and arpeggios make the use of the thumb quite easy to detect. At other times, simple hand-mechanics have dictated one choice or another. Your own skill and ear will help determine specific individual choices for right hand technique.

This book will enable you to more easily penetrate the mysterious guitar work of a man who continues to have an almost unparalleled influence on the development of popular blues-influenced music. Any correspondence can be addressed to us c/o Hal Leonard Publishing Corp., 7777 West Bluemound Rd., Milwaukee, WI 53213.

KINDHEARTED WOMAN BLUES was Robert's best rehearsed piece

– the tune he may have used to audition for H.C. Speir, and the first tune he recorded in his first session, November 23, 1936 in San Antonio. Both takes of the song were terrific and only slightly different. In the first take (transcribed here), Johnson plays the only instrumental break that he ever recorded. In the second take he omits the instrumental and sings an additional verse, "Someday, someday – I will shake your hand goodbye..." The third stanza functions musically as a bridge, establishing a very different feel and harmonic rhythm before returning to the verses.

Johnny Winter recorded this tune for Janus in the late '60s. It was also recorded by The Youngbloods and by George Thorogood and the Destroyers. Blueswoman Rory Block also recorded her version of this tune, entitled "Kindhearted Man."

Johnson is playing in standard tuning, in the key of B. He is playing 'A' figures, so I have transcribed it in the key of A. Capo to the second fret as he did to match the pitch of the original.

SA 2580-1

1. I got a kindhearted woman – do anything in this world for me.
   I got a kindhearted woman – do anything in this world for me.
   But these evil-hearted women – man, they will not let me be.
2. I love my baby – my baby don't love me.
   I love my baby, ooh – my baby don't love me.
   But I really love that woman – can't stand to leave her be.

BRIDGE: A-ain't but the one thing – makes Mr. Johnson drink,
   I's worried 'bout how you treat me, baby – I begin to think:
   Oh, babe – my life don't feel the same.
   You breaks my heart when you call Mr. So and So's name

INSTRUMENTAL BREAK

3. She's a kindhearted woman – she studies evil all the time.
   She's a kindhearted woman – she studies evil all the time.
   You well's[1] to kill me – as to have it on your mind.

ADDITIONAL VERSE FROM TAKE #SA-2580-2:

4. Someday, someday – I would shake your hand goodbye.
   Someday, someday-eee – I would shake your hand goodbye.
   I can't give you anymore of my lovin' – 'cause I just ain't satisfied.

[1] **well's:** a black colloquial contraction of 'had-just-as-well-as' that is still common in regional usage today.

Kindhearted Woman Blues

Words and Music by Robert Johnson

e-vil heart-ed wom-en, and they will not let me be.

There ain't but the one thing makes Mis-ter John-son drink. I swear by how you treat me ba-by, I be-gin to think: Oh,

babe,___ my life don't feel the same.___

You break my heart when you call___ Mis-ter so- and-so's_ name.

I Believe I'll Dust My Broom

I BELIEVE I'LL DUST MY BROOM has been Johnson's most recorded tune. From its likely origins in Kokomo Arnold's "Sagefield Woman Blues" (where he sings, "I believe, I believe I'll dust my broom"), to Elmore James' electric slide version of it in the '50s (which made it onto the national R & B charts), to versions by Canned Heat, the Spencer Davis Group, Taj Mahal, John Mayall and even Ike & Tina Turner (under the title "I Believe") this tune has a rich musical history. But what may be Johnson's most original and personal contribution to this song lies in his confidence about where his lost love will be recovered in his last verse: Ethiopia.

Ethiopia was a sort of talisman for western hemisphere Blacks during the 1920s and 1930s. Ras Tafari Makonnen had brought the country into the League of Nations in 1923, and was crowned Emperor Haile Salassie in 1930 with considerable pomp and circumstance (making the newsreel footage in the United States). Marcus Garvey's 'Back to Africa' movement was in full swing, and Ethiopia seemed a fitting model of what Black leadership could accomplish. Seeing the coronation and Selassie's eloquent championship of peace, brotherhood and the rights of the poor, weak and oppressed; many blacks in America found Ethiopia and its emperor to be a justifiable focal point for their aspirations. The emperor's alleged divinity and descent from the biblical lineage of Solomon combined with his coronation and public speeches at the League of Nations to make him the object of a Jamaican religion with distinct political overtones, whose practitioners became known as Rastafarians – after Haile Selassie's pre-coronation title and name: Ras (Prince) Tafari.

When Mussolini's Fascists invaded Ethiopia in 1935, the country became a symbol of the conflict between good and evil, a precursor of the terrible struggle about to engulf Europe and the world. In May of 1936, Haile Sellassie was driven into exile by the Italian Fascists. It was just six months after Selassie's exile, that Johnson sat down in a makeshift recording studio and sang about searching the world for some solace and relief from love's injustices – reaching as far away as China or the Philippines – somehow confident that if the symbol of this relief, his woman, could be found nowhere else, "...she must be in Ethiopia somewhere." In this brief assertion in the final line of the song, Robert personalizes and contributes to the powerful mythology of divinity, destiny and politics that Selassie and Ethiopia had come to represent. Even in the crowded and chaotic juke joints of Arkansas and Mississippi, a reference like this would not be lost.

Johnson's guitar is in open E tuning (E-B-E-G♯-B-E). The music is played and transcribed in the key of E.

SA-2581-1

1. I'm gon' get up in the mornin' – I believe I'll dust my broom.
   I'm gon' get up in the mornin' – I believe I'll dust my broom.
   Girlfriend, the black man you been lovin' –
   – girlfriend, can get my room.

2. I'm gon' write a letter – telephone every town I know.
   I'm gon' write a letter – telephone every town I know.
   If I can't find her in West Helena –
   – she must be in East Monroe, I know.

3. I don't want no woman – wants every downtown man she meet.
   I don't want no woman – wants every downtown man she meet.
   She's a no good doney[1] – they shouldn't 'low her on the street.

4. I believe – I believe I'll go back home.
   I believe – I believe I'll go back home.
   You can mistreat me here, babe – but you can't when I go home.

5. And I'm gettin' up in the mornin' – I believe I'll dust my broom.
   I'm gettin' up in the mornin' – I believe I'll dust my broom.
   Girlfriend, the black man you been lovin' –
   – girlfriend, can get my room.

6. I'm 'on' call up Chiney[2] – see is my good girl over there.
   I'm 'on' call up Chiney – see is my good girl over there.
   'f I can't find her on Philippine's Island –
   – she must be in Ethiopia somewhere.

[1] **doney/donay:** a southern variant of 'dona' which was 19th century slang for a woman. It was most likely used primarily in song rhetoric and may never have been in common use in speech. Derived from the respectful Portugese, Italian or Spanish terms for 'lady' ('Dame' and 'Prima Donna' come from the same root). It may be a term that entered into Black english from foreign slavers during the middle passage. It did not necessarily carry a negative connotation about the woman's character.

[2] **Chiney:** a phonetic transcription of Johnson's singing of 'China'.

I Believe I'll Dust My Broom

Words and Music by Robert Johnson

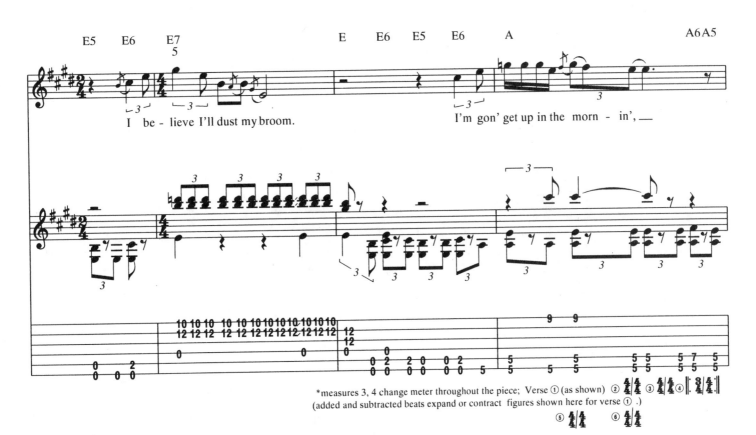

*measures 3, 4 change meter throughout the piece; Verse ① (as shown) ② ③ ④
(added and subtracted beats expand or contract figures shown here for verse ① .)
⑤ ⑥

I be- lieve I'll dust my broom._   Girl-friend, the   black men you been

lov- in', ___   girl - friend, can get   my room._

SWEET HOME CHICAGO

SWEET HOME CHICAGO was Robert's third song on Monday, November 23, 1936. Its lyrics, when taken at face value, have caused a fair amount of confusion. He sang, "Oh, baby, don't you want to go?...back to the 'land of California', to my sweet home Chicago." As with many of Johnson's images and lyrics, this seems to be not so much a matter of geographical confusion as it is a matter of his use of local/regional Black idioms.

It is possible to find a number of figures of speech persisting in black english for as much as a generation after falling out of general use in the white community. This may be have been due to a combination of factors, not limited to but including the severely restricted educational resources available to blacks and the strong oral cultures which persisted in black families and communities throughout the South.

During the middle to late 19th century, the term 'California' became synonymous with the gold rush, wealth, and money. Many a prospector rashly abandoned their homes in the East to go to California, where the gold was supposed to be just lying on the ground waiting for some lucky person to pick it up. Here Johnson seems to be inviting his woman to accompany him to a land of golden opportunity – which was not California – but for a blues musician in the 1930s, definitely *was* Chicago.

"Sweet Home Chicago" has been recorded by David Bromberg, Taj Mahal, Leon Russell & Marc Benno, The Lonnie Brooks Blues Band, and Foghat. Johnny Otis released a version of this tune under the title "Goin' Back to LA," on his ***Live At Monterey*** album.

Johnson recorded this tune in the key of F♯. His guitar is in standard tuning, and capoed at the second fret. The transcription is in E, to match his fingerings.

SA-2582-1

1. Oh, – baby, don't you want to go?
   Oh, – baby, don't you want to go?
   Back to the land of California – to my sweet home Chicago.

2. (Literal repeat of 1st Verse)

3. Now one and one is two – two and two is four,
   I'm heavy loaded, baby, – I'm booked, I got to go.
   Cryin', baby – honey, don't you want to go?
   Back to the land of California, to my sweet home Chicago.

4. Now two and two is four – four and two is six,
   You gon' keep on monkeyin' 'round here friend-boy
   you gon' get your business all in a trick, but I'm cryin'
   Baby – honey, don't you want to go?
   Back to the land of California, to my sweet home Chicago.

5. Now six and two is eight – eight and two is ten,
   Friend-boy, she trick you one time, she sure gon' do it again.
   But I'm cryin' hey, hey – baby, don't you want to go?
   To the land of California, to my sweet home Chicago.

6. I'm goin' to California – from there to Des Moines, Iowa(y) –
   Somebody will tell me that you need my help someday, cryin'
   Hey, hey – baby, don't you want to go?
   Back to the land of California, to my sweet home Chicago.

Sweet Home Chicago

Words and Music by Robert Johnson

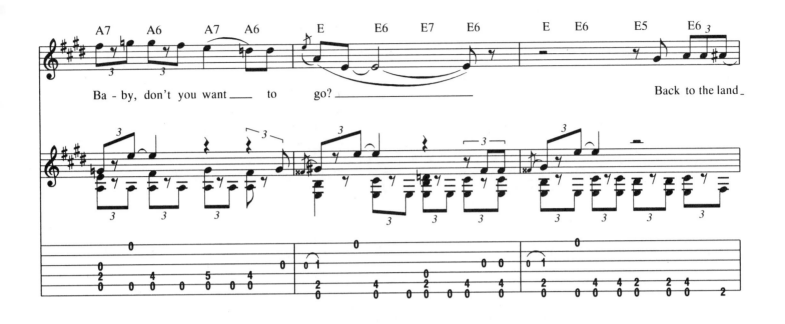

Ba - by, don't you want ___ to go? _____ Back to the land _

___ of Cal - i - for - nia   to my sweet home, ___ Chi - ca - go. ___

RAMBLIN' ON MY MIND

RAMBLIN' ON MY MIND addresses a theme that was tantalizing and at the same time, intimidating for much of the black community. The option of hitting the road when things got bad simply didn't exist for the black population during its 250 years of slavery in the South. After the Civil War, blacks, theoretically, had a right to travel, but between night-riders, sundown curfews and other Klan-inspired activities (not to mention the share-cropping system itself), freedom of movement was still restricted by the white community. Add to this the limited education and experience of most of the black sharecroppers (Robert's main audience), and we begin to appreciate the mixture of envy and fear with which they regarded traveling musicians – much as the Griot was regarded in traditional Africa. These musicians gave voice to their own frustrations, dreams and nightmares. They created a music that naturally spoke to individuals. Each listener could take the music as a personal statement.

Recorded on Johnson's first day in the studio (November 23, 1936), "Ramblin' On My Mind" quickly slipped into the musical subconscious of the Delta. Johnny Shines recorded a version of it for Chicago's JOB label in 1952. Big Joe Williams also recorded it for Milestone in 1964. John Mayall recorded it in 1966 with Eric Clapton, who recorded it again in the early '70s for a concert album.

Johnson plays it in open E-tuning (E-B-E-G♯-B-E), with a capo on the second fret – so it comes out in the key of F♯. I've transcribed it in E-tuning. You may capo on the second fret, as Johnson did, to match the pitch of the original.

SA-2583-1

1. I got ramblin' – I got ramblin' on my mind.
   I got ramblin' – I got ramblin' all on my mind.
   Hate to leave my baby – but you treats me so unkind.

2. I got mean things – I got mean things all on my mind.
   Little girl, little girl – I got means things all on my mind.
   Hate to leave you here, babe, but you treats me so unkind.

3. Runnin' down to the station – catch the first mail train I see.
   (*spoken:* 'I think I hear her comin' now')
   Runnin' down to the station – catch that old first mail train I see.
   I got the blues 'bout Miss So-and-So –
   – and the child got the blues about me.

4. And I'm leavin' this mornin' – with my arm' fold' up and cryin'.
   And I'm leavin' this mornin' – with my arm' fold' upped and cryin'.
   I hate to leave my baby – but she treats me so unkind.

5. I got mean things – I got mean things on my mind.
   I got mean things – I got mean things all on my mind.
   I got to leave my baby – well, she treats me so unkind.

ADDITIONAL VERSES FOR "RAMBLING ON MY MIND" FROM TAKE #SA-2583-2:

2. And now babe – I will never forgive you anymore.
   Little girl, little girl – I will never forgive you anymore.
   You know you did not want me – baby, why did you tell me so?

4. An' they's de'ilment — she got devilment on her mind.
   She got devilment – little girl, you got devilment all on your mind.
   Now I got to leave this mornin' – with my arm' a-fold' up and cryin'.

5. I believe – I believe my time ain't long.
   I believe – I believe that my time ain't long.
   But I'm leavin' this mornin' – I believe I will go back home.

Ramblin' On My Mind

Words and Music by Robert Johnson

Capo 2nd fret

WHEN YOU GOT A GOOD FRIEND

WHEN YOU GOT A GOOD FRIEND was recorded during Robert's first recording session on Monday, November 23, 1936. It was the fifth of eight songs Johnson mastered that day — as usual, two takes of each song were chosen and numbered in order of preference.

With only eight lines of verse, Johnson gives us an intimate portrait of a man struggling with love, pride and decision. Like almost all of Johnson's tunes, it is thematically much tighter than the bulk of the Delta blues that had been recorded previously. In 1969, Johnny Winter covered this tune for Columbia Records. It is recorded in F♯. With his guitar in standard tuning, Johnson plays E figures on the guitar with a capo on the second fret. The tune is, accordingly, transcribed in E.

SA-2584-1

1. When you got a good friend – that will stay right by your side,
   When you got a good friend – that will stay right by your side,
   Give her all of your spare time – love and treat her right.

2. I mistreated my baby – and I can't see no reason why.
   I mistreated my baby – but I can't see no reason why.
   Everytime I think about it – I just wring my hands and cry.

3. Wonder could I bear apologize – or would she sympathize with me.
   Mmmmmmmm – mmmm – mmmm – would she sympathize with me.
   She's a brownskin woman – just as sweet as a girlfriend can be.

4. Mmm-mmm – babe, I may be right or wrong.
   Baby, it's yo'(y) opinion – oh, I may be right or wrong.
   Watch your close friend, baby –
   – then you ene'ies can't do you no harm.

5. When you got a good friend – that will stay right by your side,
   When you got a good friend – that will stay right by your side,
   Give her all of your spare time-aah – love and treat her right.

When You Got A Good Friend

Words and Music by Robert Johnson

that will stay right by your side.

Give her all your spare time.____ Love ____ and treat her

right. right.

COME ON IN MY KITCHEN,

COME ON IN MY KITCHEN, one of the most darkly affecting love songs ever recorded, was cut on Johnson's first day in the studio, November 23, 1936. Johnson's lyrical first take carries a subtle threat in the last lines of its chorus that deeply affected its 1930s audience. Reminiscing about a night he and Robert played together, Johnny Shines recalled:

"One time in St. Louis we were playing one the songs that Robert would like to play with someone once in a great while, 'Come On In My Kitchen'. He was playing very slow and passionate, and when we had quit, I noticed no one was saying anything. Then I realized they were crying – both women and men."

Johnson's second take is remarkably different in text and feel, and while it is done well enough, it seems sloppy and improvised when compared to the first take. What happened to the carefully honed guitar and vocal interplay? The tight narrative pacing and the plaintive slides of the first take?

It is possible that take two (in order of the producer's preference) was recorded earlier and Robert was stretching for a different style or simply warming up. It is also possible that he was coached by the engineer or the session's producer, Don Law. While this is pure conjecture, one can almost hear them say, "That was nice Bob, but it'll never sell. Can you give it to us a little more up tempo?" It is not inconceivable that Johnson would be unsure on his first day of recording and produce this second take on his own. On the other hand, it should also be noted that the American Record Company chose to release the more chaotic take two. However it came about, we can count ourselves luck that Robert's take one survives. His legacy would be very different without it.

"Come On In My Kitchen" has been covered by many performers including David Bromberg, John Renbourn, Delaney & Bonnie, and the Steve Miller Band. Along with many others, I first heard the refrain of this tune sung by David Crosby in-between the last two cuts of the first Crosby, Stills & Nash album in 1969.

This tune is recorded in the key of B. Johnson is tuned in A-tuning (E-A-E-A-C♯-E) and capoed at the second fret, as he is for many of his bottleneck pieces. It is transcribed in the key of A with the guitar in A-tuning.

SA-2585-1

1. Mmm mmm mmm mmm – mmm mmm mmm mmm –
   Mmm mmm mmm mmm mmm – mmm mmm mmm mmm –
   You better come on in my kitchen –
   babe, it's goin' to be rainin' outdoors.

2. Ah, the woman I love – took from my best friend.
   Some joker got lucky – stole her back again.
   You better come on in my kitchen –
   Baby, it's goin' to be rainin' outdoors.

3. Oh-ah, she's gone – I know she won't come back.
   I've taken the last nickel – out of her 'nation sack[1]
   You better come on in my kitchen –
   Baby, it's goin' to be rainin' outdoors.

BRIDGE:

(*spoken*: 'Baby, can't you hear that wind howl 'n' all?'
   'Oh-y', can't you hear that wind would howl?')
      You better come on in my kitchen –
      Baby, it's goin' to be rainin' outdoors.

4. When a woman gets in trouble – everybody throws her down.
   Looking for her good friend – none can be found.
   You better come on in my kitchen –
   Baby, it's gon' to be rainin' outdoors.

5. Winter time's comin' – (h)it's gon' be slow.
   You can't make the winter, babe – that's dry long so[2]
   You better come on in my kitchen –
   'Cause it's gon' to be rainin' outdoors.

[1] **nation sack/'nation sack:** a contraction of 'donation sack'; a wallet or purse. A pouch worn by juke joint proprietors to collect proceeds for food or drink. Blues researcher Stephen Calt reported that 'nation sacks were popular among Memphis women (probably prostitutes) in the early 20th century, who wore the sacks around their waist so the money would hang down between their legs. It's also been reported that riverboat prostitutes would jingle the coins between their legs to attract customers.

[2] **dry long so:** without a reason, for no reason at all, without cause. (This is an obsolete Black colloquialism of unknown derivation.)

Come On In My Kitchen

Words and Music by Robert Johnson

gon' to be rain - in' out- doors.

2.) Ah, wom- an I *Spoken: "Baby, can't you hear the wind howl 'n' all?"*

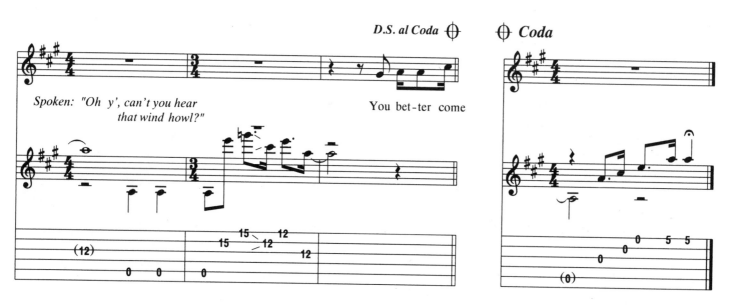

Spoken: "Oh y', can't you hear that wind howl?"

You bet-ter come

TERRAPLANE BLUES

TERRAPLANE BLUES was the seventh song on what must have been an exhausting first day of recording in San Antonio. This sexy automobile blues immediately guaranteed Johnson's place in blues history and became one of the pieces for which he was best known during his lifetime. The recording was released quickly and sold as many as 4 to 5,000 copies, a significant number in the midst of the Great Depression.

The 'Terraplane,' manufactured by the Hudson Motor Company, was one of the '30s' flashiest, low-priced cars. It had a six cylinder, 70 horsepower engine and a top speed of 88 miles per hour! "Robert didn't have one," Johnny Shines recalled, "but that was a hell of a car at the time – fast!"

Robert recorded "Terraplane Blues" in the key of B. I tuned up to A-tuning (E-A-E-A-C♯-E) and capoed to the 2nd fret for the transcriptions. Johnson probably did the same. Because of this and other tunes where he plays high on the neck with the slide ("Come On In My Kitchen," "Cross Roads," "If I Had Possession Over Judgement Day"), it is most likely that he tuned up to A, and not down to G. Further discussion of this point can be found in the notes for "Walking Blues."

John Hammond performed this tune in the PBS television tribute to his father, "The World of John Hammond." The tune was also covered by Foghat for Bearsville Records in 1975. Contemporary blues guitarist Roy Rogers has a recording available, and Rory Block recently included "Terraplane Blues" on one of her albums.

SA-2586-1

1. And I feel so lonesome – you hear me when I moan.
   And I feel so lonesome – you hear me when I moan.
   Who been drivin' my Terraplane – for you since I been gone.

2. I'd said I flash your lights, mama – your horn won't even blow.
   (*spoken:* 'Somebody's been runnin' my batteries down on this machine.')
   I even flash my lights, mama – this horn won't even blow.
   Got a short in this connection – hoo-well, babe, it's way down below.

3. I'm 'on' h'ist your hood, mama – I'm bound to check your oil.
   I'm gon' h'is your hood, mama-mmm – I'm bound to check your oil.
   I got a woman that I'm lovin' – way down in Arkansas.

BRIDGE: Now, you know the coils ain't even buzzin',
   Little generator won't get the spark.
   Motor's in a bad condition, you gotta have –
   These batt'ries charged but I'm cryin' please –
   Plea-(h)ease – don't do my wrong –.
   Who been drivin' my Terraplane now for –
   You-hoo – since I been gone.

4. Mr. Highwayman – plea-(h)ease – don't block the road.
   Puh-hee-hee-plea-(h)ease – don't block the road.
   'Cause she's re'ist'rin' a cold one hundred –
   – and I'm booked and I got to go.

5. Mmm-mmm – mmm – mmm – mmm –
   You-oo-oooo-ooo – You hear me weep and moan –.
   Who been drivin' my Terraplane now for –
   – You-hoo – since I been gone.

6. I'm 'on' get deep down in this connection –
   – keep on tanglin' with your wires.
   I'm 'on' get deep down in this connection –
   – hoo-well, keep on tanglin' with these wires.
   And when I mash down on your little starter–
   – then your spark plug will give me fire.

Terraplane Blues

Words and Music by Robert Johnson

Capo 2nd fret

you hear me when I moan. ___

Who been driv-in' my ter-ra-plane

for you since I been gone? _____

Now ya know the coils _

Bridge

_ ain't e-ven burn-ing, lit-tle gen-er-a-tor won't get the spark.

All's in a bad con-di-tion, you got-ta have _

_ these batt-'ries charged._ I'm cry-in' please, _ please! _ Don't do me wrong! _

D.S. al Coda

Who been driv-in' my ter-ra-plane for you since I been gone? _

Coda

and your spark plug 'll give_ me fire. _

PHONOGRAPH BLUES

PHONOGRAPH BLUES was the last tune of Johnson's first day in a recording studio, Monday, November 23, 1936. One take is very similar to the "Kindhearted Woman Blues" that began his session earlier in the day. The second take however, is completely different, with accompaniment almost identical to the figures he used for his song "I Believe I'll Dust My Broom"! His first take is transcribed here.

This is a marvelous song about communication, or more specifically, the lack of it "...Beatrice, she got a phonograph, but it won't say a lonesome word...What evil have I done? What evil has the poor girl heard?"

Robert returned to standard guitar tuning for his final tune of the day and capoed up two frets, making the original recording in B. In keeping with his fingerings, it is transcribed in A. You may capo, as he did, to match the pitch of the recording.

SA-2587-1

1. Beatrice, she got a phonograph – and it won't say a lonesome word.
   Beatrice, she got a phonograph – but it won't say a lonesome word.
   What evil have I done – what evil has the poor girl heard?

2. Beatrice, I love my phonograph – but you have broke my windin' chain[1].
   Beatrice, I love my phonograph – Hon'y, I broke my windin' chain.
   And you've taken my lovin' – and give it to your other man.

BRIDGE: Now, we played it on the sofa, now, we played it 'side the wall.
   My needles have got rusty, baby, they will not play at all.
   We played it on the sofa – and we played it 'side the wall.
   But my needles have got rusty – and it will not play at all.

3. Beatrice, I go crazy, baby, I will lose my mind.
   And I go cra'-ee – honey, I will lose my mind.
   Why'n't you bring your clothes back home – and try me one more time.

4. She got a phonograph – and it won't say a lonesome word.
   She got a phonograph – ooo-won't say a lonesome word.
   What evil have I done – or what evil has the poor girl heard?

[1] **windin' chain:** possibly derived from the 19th century expression for having intercourse, "to wind the clock".

Phonograph Blues

Words and Music by Robert Johnson

e - vil have I done? _____ What e - vil has the poor girl heard? ____

Verse

2.) Bea-trice, I love my pho-no-graph,_ but you have broke my wind- in' chain. _

Be-a-trice, I love my pho-no-gra-ooo. _

Hon' I broke my wind-in' chain. _____

And you've tak-en my lov - ing, _ and give it to your oth - er man.

Now, we played it on the so-fa now, we played it 'side the wall. _ My

32-20 BLUES

32-20 BLUES was the only tune Johnson recorded on November 26, 1936 during his first trip to record in San Antonio, Texas. Sandwiched in between sessions with the white gospel of The Chuck Wagon Gang and the popular Mexican musicians Andres Berlanga and Francisco Montalvo – it is Robert's version of Skip James' tune, "22-20 Blues," which was originally recorded by James in 1931 in Grafton, Wisconsin. Johnson added some new lyrics and changed the location of the tune to make it more relevant for his audience in the Delta, singing "...all the doctors in Hot Springs sure can't help her none..." He maintains the location change all the way to the eighth verse, when he slips and sings James' original "...all the doctors in Wisconsin...." It gives us a glimpse of Robert under pressure in the studio.

Johnny Winter recorded this tune in the late '60s for Janus records, including lines from Johnson's "If I Had Possession Over Judgement Day." Johnson's original recording and the transcription are both in the key of A. The guitar is in standard tuning.

SA-2616-2

1. 'F I send for my baby – and she don't come.
   'F I send for my baby – man, and she don't come.
   All the doctors in Hot Springs sure can't help her none.

2. And if she gets unruly, things she don't wan' do,
   And if she gets unruly and thinks she don't wan' do,
   Take my 32-20, now, and cut her half in two.

3. She got a .38 special but I b'lieve it's most too light.
   She got a .38 special but I b'lieve it's most too light.
   I got a 32-20, got to make the camps alright.

4. If I send for my baby, man, and she don't come.
   If I send for my baby, man, and she don't come.
   All the doctors in Hot Springs sure can't help her none.

5. I'm gonna shoot my pistol, gonna shoot my Gatling gun.
   I'm gonna shoot my pistol, got-ta shoot my Gatling gun.
   You made me love you – now your man have come.

6. Ah-oh – baby, where you stay last night?
   Ah-baby, where you stayed last night?
   You got the hair all tangled and you ain't talkin' right.

7. Her .38 special, boys, it do very well.
   Her .38 special, boys, it do very well.
   I got a 32-20 now, and it's a burnin' –.

8. If I send for my baby, man, and she don't come,
   If I send for my baby, man, and she don't come,
   All the doctors in Wisconsin sure can't help her none.

9. Hey, hey, baby, where'd you stay last night?
   Hey, hey, baby, where'd you stay last night?
   You didn't come home until the sun was shining bright.

10. Ah-oh – boy, I just can't take my rest,
    A-oh – boy, I just can't take my rest,
    With this 32-20 laying up and down my breast.

32-20 Blues

Words and Music by Robert Johnson

doc-tors in Hot Springs sure can't help — her none. _____

Verse

2.) And if she gets un - rul - y, thinks she don't — want

do. _____ If she gets un - rul - y and

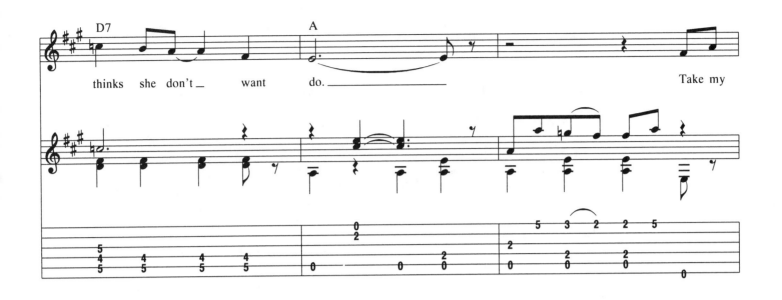

thinks she don't ‿ want do. ‿‿‿‿‿‿‿ Take my

thir - ty - two - twen - ty, now I cut her half ‿ in ‿ two. ‿

3.) She's got a east.

THEY'RE RED HOT is Robert Johnson's only uptempo 'hokum' song. It follows the chords and attitudes (and lyrics) of similar songs recorded by Tampa Red and Big Bill Broonzy, among many others. The tune is transcribed and recorded in C. For an alternate rendition of this tune, listen to John Hammond's version on his ***Mirrors*** album.

SA-2627-1

1. Hot tamales and they red hot, yes, she got 'em
   for sale.
   Hot tamales and they red hot, yes, she got 'em
   for sale.
   I got a girl, say she long and tall –
   Sleeps in the kitchen with her feets in the hall.
   Hot tamales and they red hot, yes she got 'em
   for sale, I mean –
   Yes, she got 'em for sale, yeah.

2. Hot tamales and they red hot, yes she got 'em
   for sale.
   Hot tamales and they red hot, yes she got 'em
   for sale.
   She got two for a nickel, got four for a dime–
   Would sell you more but they ain't none of mine.
   Hot tamales and they red hot, yes, she got 'em
   for sale, I mean –
   Yes, she got 'em for sale, yes, yeah.

3. Hot tamales and they red hot, yes, she got 'em
   for sale.
   Hot tamales and they red hot, yes, she got 'em
   for sale.
   I got a letter from a girl in the room –
   Now, she got somethin' good she got to bring
   home soon, now.
   It's hot tamales and they red hot, yes, she got
   'em for sale, I mean.
   Yes, she got 'em for sale, yeah.

4. Hot tamales and they red hot, yes, she got 'em
   for sale.
   Hot tamales and they red hot, yes, she got 'em
   for sale.
   (*spoken:* "They're too hot, boy!")
   The billy got back' in a bumble bee nest –
   Ever since that he can't take his rest, yeah.
   Hot tamales and they red hot, yeah, you got
   'em for sale, I mean.
   Yes, she got 'em for sale.

5. Hot tamales and they red hot, yes, she got 'em
   for sale.
   (*spoken:* "Man, don't mess around 'em, hot
         tamales, now,
              'cause they too black bad, if you –
              mess around 'em hot tamales.")
   I'm 'onna upset your backbone, put your
   kidneys to sleep –
   I'll due to break'way your liver and dare your
   heart to beat
   'bout my hot tamales 'cause they red hot –
   Yes, they got 'em for sale, I mean –
   Yes, she got 'em for sale, yeah.

6. Hot tamales and they red hot, yes, she got 'em
   for sale.
   Hot tamales and they red hot, yes, she got 'em
   for sale.
   You know grandma left, and now grandpa, too –
   Well, I wonder what in the world we chillun
   gon' do, now.
   Hot tamales and they red hot, yes, she got 'em
   for sale, I mean.
   Yes, she got 'em for sale.

7. Hot tamales and they red hot, yes, she got 'em
   for sale.
   Hot tamales and they red hot, yes, she got 'em
   for sale.
   Me and my babe, bought a V-8 Ford –
   Well, we wind that thing all on the runnin'
   board, yes.
   Hot tamales and they red hot, yes, she got 'em
   for sale, I mean.
   Yes, she got 'em for sale, yeah.

8. Hot tamales and they red hot, yes, she got 'em
   for sale.
   (*spoken:* "They too hot, boy!")
   Hot tamales and they red hot, yes, now, she
   got 'em for sale.
   You know the monkey, now the baboon
   playin' in the grass –
   Well, the monkey stuck his finger in that old
   'Good Gulf Gas', now.
   Hot tamales and they red hot, yes, she got 'em
   for sale, I mean.
   Yes, she got 'em for sale, yeah.

9. Hot tamales and they red hot, yes, she got 'em
   for sale.
   Hot tamales and they red hot, yes, she got 'em
   for sale.
   I got a girl, say she long and tall –
   Now she sleeps in the kitchen with her feets in
   the hall, yes.
   Hot tamales and they red hot, yes, now, she
   got 'em for sale, I mean.
   Yes, she got 'em for sale, yeah.

They're Red Hot

Words and Music by Robert Johnson

Introduction

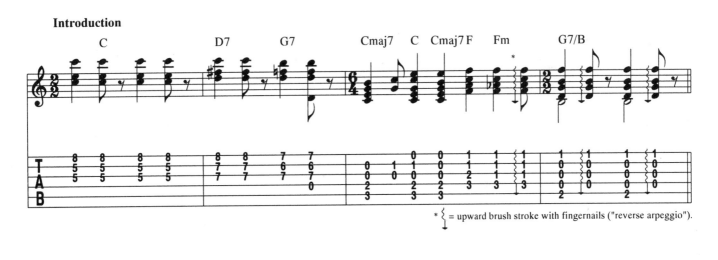

Introduction staff and tablature. Chords: C, D7, G7, Cmaj7, C, Cmaj7, F, Fm, G7/B

* ⌇ = upward brush stroke with fingernails ("reverse arpeggio").

Verse

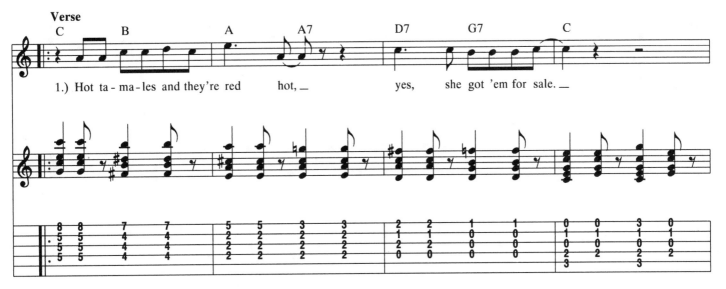

Verse staff and tablature. Chords: C, B, A, A7, D7, G7, C

1.) Hot ta- ma- les and they're red hot, — yes, she got 'em for sale. —

Staff and tablature. Chords: C, B, A, A7, D7, G7, G7/B

Hot ta- ma- les and they're red hot, — yes, she got 'em for sale. _____

I got a girl, say she long and tall, __ she sleeps in the kitch-en with her feets in the hall.

Hot ta - ma - les and they're red hot, __ yes, she got 'em for sale. __ I mean __

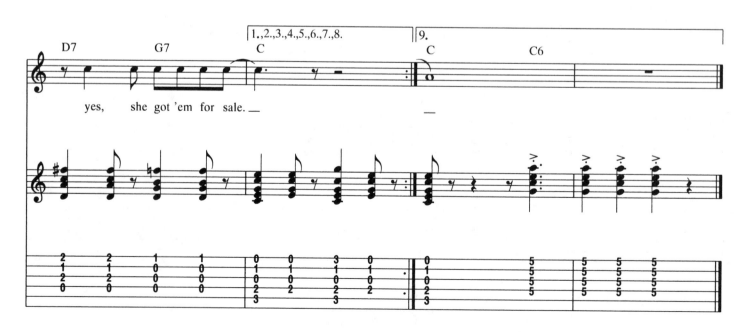

yes, she got 'em for sale. __

DEAD SHRIMP BLUES

DEAD SHRIMP BLUES was the second tune Johnson recorded (after two takes of "They're Red Hot") on Friday, November 27, 1936. Its accompaniment and structure (with the bridge section repeated this time) closely follow one of Johnson's earliest and strongest numbers, "Kindhearted Woman Blues." Both pieces are played with A figures on the guitar, and are paced similarly.

Johnson's guitar was in standard tuning and he capoed up to the second fret; making the recording in B. To match his fingerings, it is transcribed in A.

1. I woke up this morning-nnn – and all my shrimps was dead and gone.

   I woke up this mornin', ooh – all my shrimps was dead and gone.

   I was thinkin' about you, baby – why you hear me weep and moan.

2. I got dead shrimps here – someone fishin' in my pond.

   I got dead shrimps he-ooo-someone fishin' in my pond.

   I've served my best bait, baby – and I can't do that no harm.

BRIDGE Everything I do, babe, you got your mouth stuck out.

   Hole where I used to fish, you got me posted out.

   Everything I do – you got your mouth stuck out.

   At the hole where I used to fish, baby,

   – you got me posted out.

3. I got dead shrimps here, 'n' someone fishin' in my pond.

   I got dead shrimps here — someone fishin' in my pond.

   Catchin' my goggle-eyed perches – and they barbecuin' the bone.

BRIDGE Now you take my shrimp, baby – you know you turned me down.

   I couldn't do nothin' until I got myself unwound.

   You taken my shrimp – ooh, know you turned me down.

   Babe, I couldn't do nothin' – until I got myself unwound.

Dead Shrimp Blues

Words and Music by Robert Johnson

Capo 2nd fret

*Mute downstems (bass strings) only.

some-one fish-in' in my pond.

I've served _ my best bet, ba - by, _____ and I can't do that no harm. _

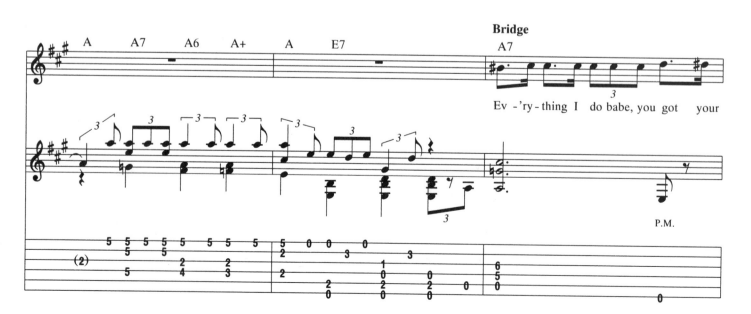

Ev -'ry-thing I do babe, you got your

P.M.

CROSS ROAD BLUES

CROSS ROAD BLUES was recorded in San Antonio on Friday, November 27, 1936. With much of its opening statement mixing measures of three with measures of four, Johnson seemed determined to keep the listener off-balance – in an almost intoxicated state of vigilance – waiting for the beat to settle down into four (which it does finally, though he continues to use added beats and shortened measures within the tune). This rhythmic uncertainty accentuates the listener's own sense of the unpredictable and often dangerous situation described in the lyrics.

Many counties in Mississippi had sundown curfews on blacks, possibly to curtail the very activities Johnson and other musicians were helping to create: juke joint, late-night drinking and gambling, where an intoxicating mix of alcohol, sex, music and being out-of-sight of the white community often led to jealous violence and mayhem. Johnson himself was to become a victim of just such violence.

To find one's self on the roadside with the sun quickly vanishing – its last rays foreshadowing the long night ahead – was a forbidding prospect that many musicians had to face. Laced with highway sound effects and insistent, unsettling rhythms, Johnson's guitar part crackles with this sense of danger and foreboding.

Johnson's own murder in 1938 was not even reported to the LeFlore County sheriff's office until 1970, when researcher Mack McCormick tried to provide them with the names and addresses of witnesses to the murder. They didn't even bother to take down the information. Murdered blacks – whether killed by whites *or* blacks – were still invisible victims to the white law establishment: as invisible as Robert sang of being while standing at the cross road when everybody passed him by.

Covered by Eric Clapton and the rock group Cream in the late '60s, "Cross Road Blues" became a signature piece for a generation. It has been covered by many artists, from Stephen Stills, Clapton, John Hammond and Lynyrd Skynyrd, to Ry Cooder (for the sound track to the movie ***Crossroads***). Rory Block also has a recording available, and Windham Hill has released a version of "Cross Road Blues" by the Turtle Island String Quartet!

This tune is recorded in the key of B, with the guitar in A-tuning (E-A-E-A-C♯-E) and a capo at the second fret. It is transcribed in the key of A. A capo should be placed at the second fret to match the recordings. A note should be mentioned about the barlines: grouping beats in Johnson's more complicated pieces can be pretty arbitrary. In "Cross Road Blues," we have some guidance from the worksong structures to which it is related. Like "Walking Blues" (see notes for additional information), this tune is related to worksongs (axe songs) in which the downbeat of the measure was generally left empty to facilitate unison chopping, spike driving, etc. The barlines and measure lengths have been set with this in mind. It is important to note that when Johnson added or dropped beats, he did not alter the feeling of the measure – 3/4 never is played like a waltz; 5/4 is a 4/4 measure that goes on for one extra beat.

SA-2629-1

1. I went to the cross road – fell down on my knee.
   I went to the cross road – fell down on my knee.
   I asked the Lord above, "Have mercy —"
   Save poor Bob, if you please."

2. Mmmmmmm — standin' at the cross road – I tried to flag a ride.
   Standin' at the cross road — I tried to flag a ride.
   Didn't nobody seem to know me – everybody pass me by.

3. Mmm – the sun goin' down, boy – dark gon' catch me here.
   Ooooo-eeee – boy, dark gon' catch me here.
   I haven't got no lovin' sweet woman that –
   – love and feel my care.

4. You can run – you can run – tell my friend-boy, Willie Brown.
   You can run – tell my friend-boy, Willie Brown.
   Lord, that I'm standin' at the cross road, babe –
   – I believe I'm sinkin' down.

Cross Road Blues

Words and Music by Robert Johnson

Capo 2nd fret

Asked the Lord a-bove, "Have mer-cy, _____

save _ poor _ Bob, _ if you please." _

2.) Mmm, _ stand-in' at the cross - road, _

I tried _ to flag a _ ride. _

Stand-in' at the cross-

- road _____ I _ tried_ to flag a __ ride. __

Did– n't no–bod– y   seem to know me,   ev–'ry – bod–y   pass me by. _____

w/slide   w/fingers

3.) Mmm,_ the sun __ go – in' down boys, __   dark_ gon' catch me here. __

Falsetto: Ooo,— oo - ee, ee——— boy, dark gon' catch me here.—

—— I have-n't got no lov-in' sweet wom-an that— love

and feel my— care.——— 4.) You can run,—

WALKING BLUES shows Robert's debt to Son House more clearly than any other piece. Inspired by House's "My Black Mama," it was recorded in San Antonio during Robert's first trip to record for ARC, three days after his initial session. (In the interim ARC had recorded a pair of guitar-playing Mexican sisters, the Hermanas Barraza, and a white gospel group, the Chuck Wagon Gang.)

This song, like many other blues (and later, rock 'n' roll) songs has its roots in the rhythms of work songs that were used continuously from slave times up through Reconstruction and preserved on the prison workfarms. "Walking Blues" is an example of an 'axe song'. This type of song was also used by crews laying railroad track, or by any group working in rhythm. Two lines of men would face each other with the log or rail between them and take turns swinging their axes or hammers. The downbeat of the lines of the song was left empty so that the hammers or axes could fall on the first beat of the measure and the work could progress in a safe, coordinated fashion.

The rhythmic drive and themes in "Walking Blues" have made it one of Johnson's most popular tunes, with covers by Paul Butterfield, Taj Mahal, Johnny Winter, and Bonnie Raitt. It has also been recorded by Muddy Waters, the Grateful Dead, the Hindu Love Gods and Rory Block.

Johnson recorded this tune in the key of B, with his guitar tuned up to A-tuning (E-A-E-A-C♯-E) and a capo on the second fret. This made the high slide work easier on the 12-fret neck that was standard in the '30s, and also maintained the higher tension necessary to keep string noise down when the guitar is hit hard. To preserve his fingerings, I have transcribed the tune in the key of A and in open A-tuning. You may capo up to match the pitch of the recording.

SA-2630-1

1. I woke – up this mornin' – feelin' 'round for my shoes.
   Know 'bout 'at I got these – old walkin' blues. Woke –
   Up this mornin' – feelin' 'round all for my shoes.
   But you know 'bout 'at I – got these old walkin' blues.

2. Lord, I – feel like blowin' my – woh-old lonesome home.
   Got up this mornin', my little Ber-nice was gone, Lord.
   I feel like — blow-ooowin' my lonesome home.
   Well, I got up this mornin' — woh-all I had was gone.

3. Well-ah — leave this morn' if I have to – woh, ride the blind[1]-ah.
   I feel mistreated and I – don't mind dyin' –
   Leavin' this morn'-ah – 'f I have to ride a blind.
   Babe, I been mistreated – baby, and I don't mind dyin'.

4. Well, — some people tell me that the worried – blues ain't bad.
   Worst old feelin' I most – ever had –
   Some – people tell me that these – old worried, old blues ain't bad.
   It's the worst old feelin' – I – most ever had.

5. She got a – Elgin movement[2] from her head down – to her toes.
   Break in on a dollar most any – where she goes,
   Ooooo-ooo – From her head down to her toes – (*spoken:* 'Oh, honey')
   Lord, she break in on a dollar – most anywhere she goes.

[1] **ride the blind:** to hop a train; hoboing.

[2] **Elgin movement:** a reference to the well-made, smooth working inner movement of the watch by the same name.

Walking Blues

Words and Music by Robert Johnson

But you _ know _____ 'bout 'at _ I _____

1.,2.,3.,4.

2.) Lord, I

(goes). _

LAST FAIR DEAL GONE DOWN

LAST FAIR DEAL GONE DOWN was the fifth song Johnson recorded on November 27, 1936 (following "They're Red Hot," "Dead Shrimp Blues," "Cross Road Blues," and "Walkin' Blues"). In this and his other uptempo A-tuning pieces, with their frantic rhythmic pace and title themes, we have some of Johnson's most direct antecedents of rock 'n' roll. Had Robert survived another 3 or 4 months to take part in John Hammond, Sr.'s "From Spirituals to Swing" Concert in Carnegie Hall, the rock 'n' roll era could have begun 15 years earlier.

In the lyrics Robert refers to Gulfport, Mississippi. Located on the Gulf of Mexico, Gulfport was the southern terminus of the Gulfport Island Railroad which ran north through the Delta to Memphis and served as a major source of transportation for musicians when they decided to jump a train or "ride the blind." The fifth verse of this song has long defied transcribers: it is a verse where the guitar accompaniment is abbreviated and choked – and Johnson's inscrutable lyrics are sung in a similar fashion. I included what I think he is singing here, but a phonetic transcription might have been safer.

At the end of the piece, Johnson's evokes the sound of bells with guitar harmonics – pausing to make the emphasis. The recording is in the key of A and is transcribed in A, as well. It is played in open A-tuning (E-A-E-A-C♯-E), with a slide on the fourth finger.

SA-2631-1

1. It's the last fair deal goin' down – last fair deal goin' down,
   It's the last fair deal goin' down, good Lord,
   On that Gulfport Island Road.

2. Eh, Ida Belle, don't cry this time – Ida Belle don't cry this time.
   If you cry about a nickel – you'll die 'bout a dime
   She wouldn't cry – but the money won't[1] mine.

3. I love the way you do – I love the way you do –
   I love the way you do, good Lord –
   On this Gulfport Island Road.

4. My captain's so mean on me – My captain's so mean on me –
   My captain's so mean on m'-mmmmm, good Lord –
   On this Gulfport Island Road.

5. 'E' 'calp a bi' and si' – 'calp a bi' and si' –
   Le's scalp a bit and sing, good Lord –
   On that Gulfport Island Road.[2]

6. Ah, this last fair deal goin' down –
   –it's the last fair deal goin' down.
   This' the last fair deal goin' down, good Lord –
   On this Gulfport Island Road.

7. I'm workin' my way back home – I'm workin' my way back home –
   I'm workin' my way back home, good Lord –
   On this Gulfport Island Road.

8. And that thing don't keep a-ringin' so soon –
   – that thing don't keep a-ringin' so soon –
   And that thing don't keep a-ringin' so soon, good Lord –
   On that Gulf(ed) and Port Island Road.

[1] **won't:** a colloquial substitution for 'weren't'.

[2] The 5th verse lyrics are really up for grabs. If the lyrics here are substantially correct, Johnson's reference to scalping may be related to another Delta expression, "getting your head cut," which was employed when a musician was flamboyantly outplayed by another musician and consequently lost the attention (and the tips) of the crowd. The winner of the spontaneous competition was said to have cut the loser's head and the loser was essentially 'finished.'

Last Fair Deal Gone Down

Words and Music by Robert Johnson

5.) 'calp a bi'___ and si', 'calp a bi'___ and si'._____ Le's

scalp_____ a bit_____ and sing,___ good Lord,___ on this Gulf - port Is - land

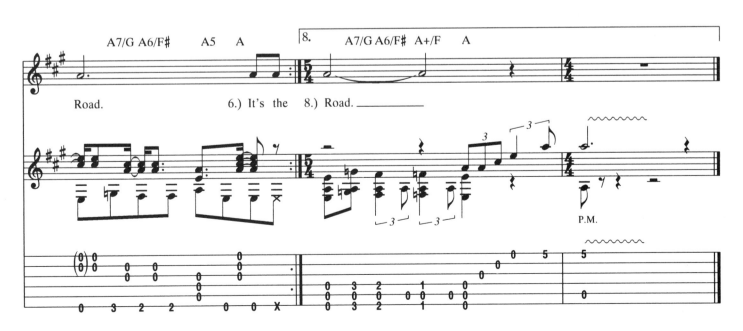

Road.   6.) It's the   8.) Road._____

PREACHING BLUES

PREACHING BLUES (Up Jumped The Devil) is Robert's revision of Son House's "Preachin' Blues" (which Son recorded for Paramount Records in Grafton, Wisconsin, in the summer of 1930). Robert's early exposure to the seasoned, impassioned playing of the older musician comes through here not just in this extension on the musical material (a part of both the traditional and original aspects of Johnson's music), but also in the frenzied intensity of Robert's performance. Only one take survives.

The recording and transcription are both in the key of E. Robert had his guitar in E-tuning (E-B-E-G♯-B-E) and played without a capo.

SA-2632-1

1. Mmmmmm – mmmm –
   I's up this mornin' – ah, blues walkin' like a man.
   I's up this mornin' – ah, blues walkin' like a man.
   Worried blues – give me your right hand.

2. And the blues fell mama's child – tore me all upside down.
   Blues fell mama's child – and it tore me all upside down.
   Travel on, poor Bob – just can't turn you 'round.

3. The blu-(h)u-u-ues – is low-down shakin' chill.
   (*spoken:* 'Yes, preach 'em now.')
   Mmmmmmm-mmmm – is a low-down shakin' chill.
   You ain't neve' had 'em – I—hope you never will.

4. Well, the blues – is an achin' old heart disease.
   (*spoken:* 'Do it now. You gonna do it? Tell me all about it')
   Let the blues – is a low-down achin' heart disease.
   Like consumption – killin' me by degrees.

5. I did start 'er r-rain[1] – oh, oh, drive – oh, oh, drive my blues –
   I did start 'er r-rainin' – I'm 'on' drive my blues away.
   Goin' to the 'still'ry[2] – stay out there all day.

[1] **'start 'er r-rainin':** This is another tough verse to make out. Johnson may also be singing 'stutter-r(a)-ing,' which he then illustrates throughout the verse.

[2] **'still'ry:** Distillery

Preaching Blues (Up Jumped The Devil)

Words and Music by Robert Johnson

*Upstems played with slide throughout.

blues   walk-in' like a man. ___

Wor-ried blues, ___   give me ___ your ___ right ___ hand. ___

*Palm mute on downstems only.

2.) And the blues ___

If I had Possession Over Judgement Day

With its threat of sexual damnation, ("...any woman didn't want no lovin' – wouldn't have no right to pray...") this tune was simply too hot to be released in the 1930's and was first heard when Columbia issued its first volume of Johnson's recordings in 1962.

The guitar part is derived from "Roll and Tumble Blues" – a widely imitated piece that was a standard of the Delta repertoire. Robert's version draws a verse from Son House's "My Black Woman" ("...Had to fold my arms and I slowly walked away...") Along with the borrowed lyrics, the impassioned singing and Johnson's stratospheric slide work in the last verse also seem to owe a debt to Son's passionate style. This high slide work seems to verify that Robert's guitar must have been in A-tuning for this as well as his other slide pieces.

John Hammond and Sparky Rucker have both recorded versions of this tune. Johnny Winter borrowed lyrics for his version of Johnson's "32-20 Blues" in the late 1960s. Johnson's recording and the transcription are both in the key of A. The guitar is tuned to open A-tuning (E-A-E-A-C♯-E).

SA-2633-1

1. If I had possession over judgment day,
   If I had possession over judgement day,
   Lord, the little woman I'm lovin' wouldn't –
   – have no right to pray.

2. And I went to the mountain – lookin' far as my eyes could see.
   And I went to the mountain – lookin' far as my eyes could see.
   Some other man got my woman and the '-a –
   – lonesome blues got me.

3. And I rolled and I tumbled and I – cried the whole night long.
   And I rolled and I tumbled and I – cried the whole night long.
   Boy, I woke up this mornin' – my biscuit roller gone.

4. Had to fold my arms and I – slowly walked away –
   (*spoken:* 'I didn't like the way she done.')
   Had to fold my arms and I – slowly walked away –
   I said in my mind, "Yo' trouble gon' come someday."

5. Now run here, baby – set down on my knee –
   Now run here, baby – set down on my knee –
   I wanna tell you all about the – way they treated me.

If I Had Possession Over Judgement Day

Words and Music by Robert Johnson

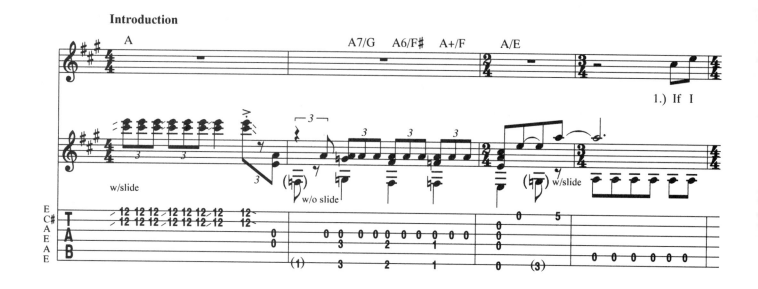

had pos-ses-sion   o - ver judge - ment day.____

Lord,   they   did-n't want no lov-in', __ would-n't

have no right _ to   pray. ____

2.) And I went to the moun - tain and it burned my eyes _ to see. _

And I went to the moun - tain and it burned my eyes _ to see. _

STONES IN MY PASSWAY was recorded on Saturday, June 19, 1937.

The American Record Company (ARC) had set up a make-shift studio on the third floor of the office building that served as the distribution point for Brunswick Records in downtown Dallas. The sessions were scheduled for Saturday and Sunday, probably to try and avoid the weekday street noise. Even so the windows were kept closed, and it quickly became unbearably hot. Blocks of ice were set up with fans to blow over them between takes to try to keep the temperature down, but the attempt was only marginally successful.

'Stones' signaled Johnson's return to the studio after a hiatus of nearly seven months. Robert was able to record just two other numbers before making room for "Zeke Williams & His Rambling Cowboys." He returned in the middle of the following day to record ten more selections. To appreciate the length of the recording day, consider that, in addition to Johnson's ten songs (represented by 23 takes, it is likely more were made and discarded), the engineers recorded five other bands and a vanity recording of another soloist! Of these last thirteen recordings, Robert had eleven released within the next year. But in less than fourteen months, Johnson was dead.

This is another slide piece in open A-tuning (E-A-E-A-C♯-E). The recording and transcription are both in the key of A. For an alternate version, listen to John Hammond on his 1967 album ***Mirrors.***

DAL-377-2

1. I got stones in my passway – and my road seem dark as night.
   I got stones in my passway – and my road seem dark as night.
   I have pains in my heart – they have taken my appetite.
2. I have a bird to whistle – and I have a bird to sing.
   Have a bird to whistle – and I have a bird to sing.
   I got a woman that I'm lovin' – boy, but she don't mean a thing.
3. My enemies have betrayed me – have overtaken poor Bob at last.
   My enemies have betrayed me – have overtaken poor Bob at last.
   An' 'ere's one thing certainly – they have stones all in my pass.
BRIDGE: Now you tryin' to take my life, – And all my lovin', too.
   You laid a passway for me – now what are you tryin' to do?
   I'm cryin', "Please – plea-ease, let us be friends.
   And when you hear me howlin' in my passway, rider –
   Plea-ease open your door and let me in.
4. I got three legs to truck home – boys, please don't block my road.
   I got three legs to truck home – boys, please don't block my road.
   I've been feelin' ashamed 'bout my rider –
   – babe, I'm booked and I got to go.

Stones In My Passway

Words and Music by Robert Johnson

I have   pains in my heart, —

they have tak-en my ap-pe-tite. —

2.) I have a

Now you try'ng to take my life, —

I'M A STEADY ROLLIN' MAN

I'M A STEADY ROLLIN' MAN is one of the great traveling blues. Johnson cut this on Saturday, June 19, 1937. It was issued on the ARC, Vocalion and Conqueror labels before it was re-issued on Columbia's *Robert Johnson: King of the Delta Blues, Vol. II* in 1971. The original recording is in the key of B-flat. Johnson is in standard tuning, with the capo on the first fret, playing A figures. The transcription is, accordingly, in the key of A.

"I'm A Steady Rollin' Man" was recorded by Eric Clapton on his *461 Ocean Boulevard* album.

DAL-378-1

1. I'm a steady rollin' man – I roll both night and day.

   I'm a steady rollin' man – hmm, hmm, I roll both night and day.

   But I haven't got no sweet woman –

   – hmm, hmm, boys, to be rollin' this a-way

2. I'm the man that rolls when icicles is hangin' on the tree.

   I'm the man that rolls when icicles is hangin' on the tree.

   And now you hear me howlin', baby –

   – hmm, hmm, mmm, down on my bended knee.

3. I'm a hard workin' man – have been for many years, I know.

   I'm a hard workin' man – have been for many long years, I know.

   And some cream puff's[1] usin' my money –

   – ooh, well, babe, but that'll never be no more.

4. You can't give your sweet woman – everything she wants in one time.

   Ooh, hoo-ooo, You can't give your sweet woman –

   – everything she wants in one time.

   Well, boys, she get ramblin' in her brain, hmm, mm, mmm –

   – some monkey man[2] on her mind.

5. I'm a steady rollin' man – I roll both night and day.

   I am a steady rollin' man – and I roll both night and day.

   Well, I don't have no sweet woman –

   – hmm, mmm, boys, to be rollin' this a-way.

[1] **cream puff:** a pejorative term for a male consort, a dandy.

[2] **monkey man:** a man who sneaks around and sleeps with another man's woman on the sly, a backdoor man. Alternately, a weak-willed man who always does just what his woman wants.

I'm A Steady Rollin' Man

Words and Music by Robert Johnson

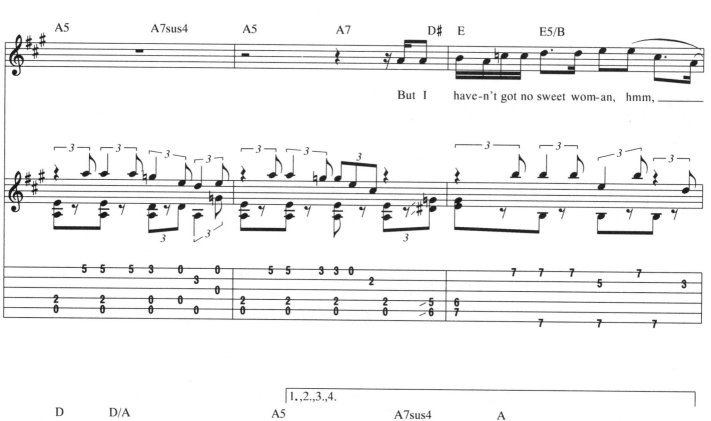

But I have-n't got no sweet wom-an, hmm,

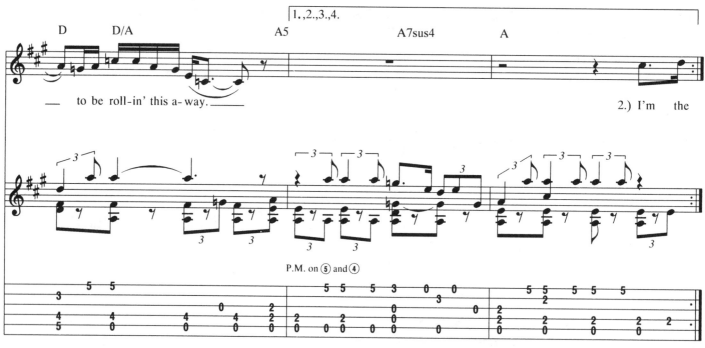

to be roll-in' this a-way. 2.) I'm the

FROM FOUR TILL LATE

FROM FOUR TILL LATE seems to have its roots in a musical style from outside of the Delta region. Gone is the raw, emotional singing style characteristic of Delta blues singers. In the place of the now-classic highly rhythmic accompaniments, we find Johnson's arrangement more in line with the ragtime piano influenced sounds of Piedmont blues.

The wide range of Johnson's travels and his chameleon-like ability to adopt diverse guitar styles and recall new material seem evident in this tune. In the opening verse, Robert seems to be headed for the southern terminus of the Gulfport Island railroad in Gulfport, MS, on the Gulf of Mexico. In the second verse, he mentioned that it was a 36 hour ride between Memphis and Norfolk, a trip of approximately 800 miles. This triangle of locations, from Memphis to Gulfport and Norfolk, articulates the boundaries of the entire southeast. If Johnson is talking about driving straight through on the Memphis to Norfolk run – his average speed would only be 22 miles per hour! He is playing in standard tuning. The piece is transcribed in its original key.

"From Four Till Late" has also been recorded by Eric Clapton with Cream and by acoustic bluesman John Hammond.

DAL-379-1

1. From four 'ntil late, I was wringin' my hands and cryin'.
   From four 'ntil late, I was wringin' my hands and cryin'.
   I believe to my soul that your daddy's Gulfport bound.

2. From Memphis to Norfolk is a thirty-six hours' ride.
   From Memphis to Norfolk is a thirty-six hours' ride.
   A man is like a prisoner and he's never satisfied.

3. A woman is like a dresser – some man always ramblin' th'ough its drawers.
   A woman is like a dresser – some man's always ramblin' th'ough its drawers –.
   It cause' so many men – wear an apron overall.

4. From four 'ntil late she get with a no good bunch and clown.
   From four 'ntil late she get with a no good bunch and clown.
   Now, she won't do nothin' but tear a good man reputation down.

5. When I leave this town – I'm 'on' bid you fare – farewell.
   When I leave this town – I'm gon' bid you fare – farewell.
   And when I return again, you'll have a great long story to tell.

From Four Till Late

Words and Music by Robert Johnson

I be - lieve ___ to my soul ___ that your dad -

- dy's ___ Gulf - port ___ bound. ___

2.) From Mem -

Verse

phis to Nor - folk is a thir - ty - six hour ___ drive. ___

*Rap guitar body with fingernail.

HELLHOUND ON MY TRAIL

HELLHOUND ON MY TRAIL began Johnson's last day of recording, June 20, 1937. It couldn't have been an accident that this was how Robert decided to start off his Sunday morning. While the rest of the community was gathered in churches hoping to save their souls, Robert was seeking his salvation in a recording studio where the recording crew had tried to beat the heat by getting an early start on the day.

Blues and gospel music have often seemed to address the same concern – the survival of our spirit in what is too often a brutal and forbidding world. And while the church focused on some future salvation in another realm, bluesmen and women seemed bound up with the living, unable or unwilling to look beyond the grave. And so their comfort and hope of salvation often lay between them – men and women clinging to one another with such desperate expectations that it would have been almost impossible for any love to survive for long. "Hellbound On My Trail" must have seemed like a fitting testament on that sweltering Sunday in Dallas as Robert opened his guitar case and tuned up for what was to be his last session.

Other versions of this tune have been recorded by Fleetwood Mac and blues guitarist John Hammond.

Johnson's guitar is in open E-tuning (E-B-E-G♯-B-E). The tune is recorded and transcribed in the key of E. Unlike most of his other songs in open tunings, Robert refrained from using a slide on this one. Instead he used bends to achieve a similar effect.

DAL-394-2

1. I got to keep movin' – I got to keep movin' –
   Blues fallin' down like hail.
   Blues fallin' down like hail.
   Ummm–, mmm, mmm, mmmm–
   Blues fallin' down like hail.
   Blues fallin' down like hail.
   And the day keeps on my knee[1] – It's a hellhound on my trail.
   Hellhound on my trail –
   Hellhound on my trail –

2. If today was Christmas Eve – if today was Christmas Eve –
   And tomorrow was Christmas Day,
   If today was Christmas Eve –
   And tomorrow was Christmas Day,
   (*spoken:* Aow, wouldn't we have a time, baby?)
   All I would need my little sweet rider just –
   To pass the time away, uh-uh –
   To pass the time away.

3. You sprinkle hot foot powder[2], mmmm –
   Mmmm – around my door,
   All around my door.
   You sprinkle hot foot powder –
   All around your daddy's door,
   hmmm, hmm, hmm–
   It keep me with a ramblin' mind, rider –
   Every old place I go.
   Every old place I go.

4. I can tell the wind is risin' –
   The leaves are tremblin' on the tree –
   Tremblin' on the tree –.
   I can tell the wind is risin' –
   leaves tremblin' on the tree,
   Hmm, hmm, hmm, mmmm –
   All I need's my little sweet woman –
   And to keep my company,
   Hmmm, hmm, mmm, mmmm –
   My company.

[1] **And the day keeps on my knee:** This line may also be "And the day keeps worryin' me –"

[2] **hot foot powder:** 'Doctor Pryor's Alleged Hot Foot Powder – for burning or sprinkling' is still manufactured by Japo Oriental Incense Co., Chicago 21, IL.

Hellhound On My Trail

Words and Music by Robert Johnson

Introduction

Verse

Chris'- mas Eve, _ and to- mo'ow was _ Chris'- mas Day. _ If to-day _

_ was Chris'- mas Eve _____ and to-mo'ow was Chris'- mas Day, _____ (*Spoken:* "Oh, wouldn't we have a time, baby...") all I would

need my lit-tle sweet rid-er just to pass the time a - way. Huh,_ huh,_ to pass the time a-way. _

LITTLE QUEEN OF SPADES

LITTLE QUEEN OF SPADES was released, with "Me and the Devil Blues" on the flip side, of Vocalion #04108. Recorded with the guitar in standard tuning, it is transcribed in its original key. As in "Terraplane Blues," Johnson has chosen a metaphor (cards and gambling) and milked it of its sexual potential. This tune seems to be the direct thematic antecedent of Stephen Stills' acoustic tour-de-force, "Black Queen."

DAL-395-2

1. Mmmm–, she is a little queen of spades –
   – and the men will not let her be.
   Hoo, hoo-oo, she is the little queen of spades –
   – and the men will not let her be.
   Everytime she makes a spread –
   Hoo – cold chill just runs all over me.

2. 'ell, I'm gon' get me a gamblin' woman –
   – 'f i's the last thing that I do.
   Ooo, hoo-eee – gon' get me a gamblin' woman –
   – 'f i's the last thing that I do.
   A man don't need a woman –
   – Hoo, fair brown, he got to give all of his money to.

3. 'ell, everybody say she got a mojo[1], –
   – baby, you've been usin' that stuff.
   Hmmm, hmmm – mmmm – everybody say she got a mojo –
   – 'cause she been usin' that stuff.
   She got a way 'tremblin' down[2] –
   – hoo we', babe, and I mean it's most too tough.

4. Well, well, little girl, since I am the King –
   – fair brown, and you is a queen.
   Hoo, hoo – ooee – since I am the king –
   – baby, and you is a queen.
   Le's we put our heads together –
   – hoo, fair brown, then we can make our money green.

[1] **mojo:** a conjurer's charm to give the owner power over others, to cause them harm, or to make the owner sexually irresistible to them. In this tune, it seems to be used to communicate both these uses.

[2] **tremblin' down:** this is a euphemism for sexual intercourse.

Little Queen Of Spades

Words and Music by Robert Johnson

Introduction

Verse

*Palm mute used on downstems only throughout.

MALTED MILK and "Drunken Hearted Man" share a passive melancholia that is not found in Johnson's more original work. Along with shared thematic associations with alcohol, Johnson's sad, dream-like vocal quality and use of dropped-D tuning (D-A-D-G-B-E) mark these tunes as derivations in the style of Lonnie Johnson's early recordings. Borrowing the last verse from Lonnie Johnson's 1927 recording of "Blue Ghost Blues," Robert bows his head to the muse that sired "Hellhound On My Trail" and "Me and the Devil Blues," and what would be a maudlin little number takes on some of the darkness of superstition – a touch of voodoo.

"Malted Milk" is transcribed in the key of D. To match the pitch of the original recording, simply capo up one fret to the key of E-flat.

DAL-396-1

1. I keep drinkin' malted milk[1] – tryin' to drive my blues away.
   I keep drinkin' malted milk – tryin' to drive my blues away.
   But you just as welcome to my lovin' – as the flowers is in May.

2. Malted milk, malted milk – keep rushin' to my head.
   Malted milk, malted milk – keep rushin' to my head.
   And I have a funny, funny feelin' – and I'm talkin' all out my head.

3. Baby, fix me one more drink – and hug your daddy one more time.
   Baby, fix me one more drink – and hug your daddy one more time.
   Keep on stirrin' in my malted milk, mama – until I change my mind.

4. My doorknob keeps on turnin' – it must be spooks around my bed.
   My doorknob keeps on turnin' – must be spooks around my bed.
   I have a warm, old feelin' – and the hair risin' on my head.

[1] **malted milk:** according to Robinsonville musician Willie Moore that was the local, Depression-era slang for beer.

Malted Milk

Words and Music by Robert Johnson

Ba-by, you just as wel-come to my lov-in' _ as the flow - ers is in May. _

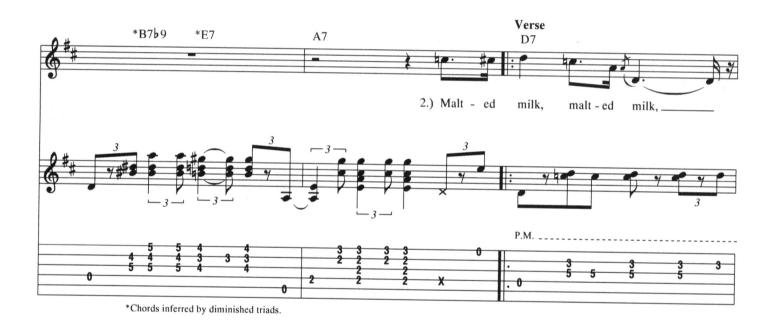

2.) Malt - ed milk, malt - ed milk, _____

*Chords inferred by diminished triads.

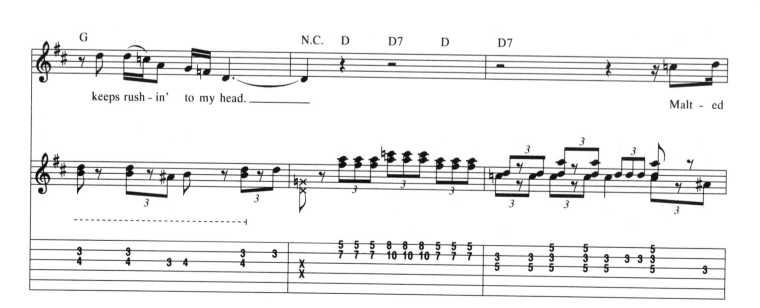

keeps rush - in' to my head. _____

Malt - ed

DRUNKEN HEARTED MAN

DRUNKEN HEARTED MAN was cut during Johnson's last recording session (Sunday, June 20, 1937) in Dallas, TX. The recording is in the key of E-flat, but Robert's guitar is in dropped-D tuning (D-A-D-G-B-E), with a capo at the 1st fret. The piece shows more clearly than any other in Johnson's repertoire the influence of Lonnie Johnson's recordings. Lonnie Johnson's complete mastery of this tuning and his agility as a blues-jazz crossover guitarist kept him in demand as a sideman in jazz oriented ensembles and as a solo blues artist. It has been reported that Robert would occasionally characterize himself as "one of those Johnson boys," taking whatever advantage could be had by associating himself with the widely-known, older musician. Lonnie Johnson recorded a piece entitled "Broken Levee Blues," in which he sings about the dangerous labor forced on Delta Blacks when the Mississippi was in flood stage. This 'levee blues' of Lonnie Johnson's has accompaniment figures identical to those heard throughout "Drunken Hearted Man." If the laconic vocals and guitar figures of this piece interest you, you should check out Lonnie Johnson (his solo and duet recordings are the most inspiring).

DAL-397-2

1. I'm a drunken hearted man – my life seem so misery.
   I'm the drunken hearted man – my life seem so misery.
   And if I could only change my way of livin' –
   – it t'would mean so much to me.
2. I been dogged and I been driven – eve' since I left my mother's home.
   I been dogged and I been driven – eve' since I left my mother's home.
   And I cant see the reason why –
   that I can't leave these no good womens alone.
3. My poor father died and left me and my mother done the best that she could.
   My poor father died and left me – and my mother done the best that she could.
   Every man love that game you call love –
   – but it don't mean no man no good.
4. I'm the poor drunken hearted man and sin was the cause of it all.
   I'm a poor drunken hearted man – and sin was the cause of it all.
   But the day you get weak for no good women –
   that's the day that you surely fall.

Drunken Hearted Man

Words and Music by Robert Johnson

*This 2/4 bar is omitted in subsequent verses.

*See 3rd Verse variant.

*see variants for 2nd and 4th Verses.

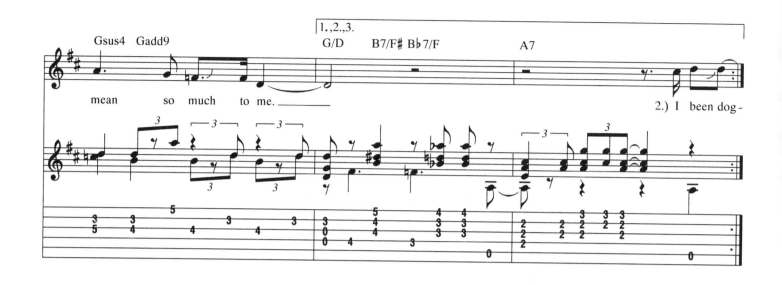

Gsus4 Gadd9   1.,2.,3.   G/D   B7/F♯   B♭7/F   A7

mean   so   much   to   me. _____   2.) I been dog-

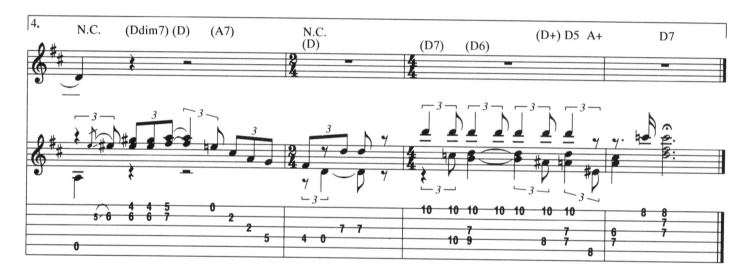

4.   N.C.   (Ddim7) (D)   (A7)   N.C.(D)   (D7)   (D6)   (D+) D5 A+   D7

2nd Verse Variant

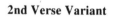

N.C.(Dm)   (Em)   (Ddim7) D   D5/7

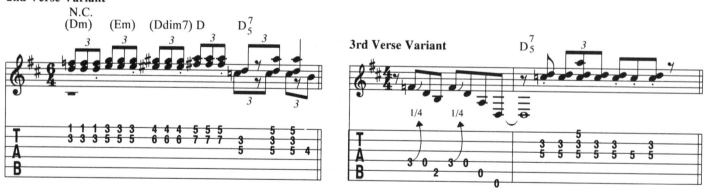

3rd Verse Variant   D5/7

4th Verse Variant

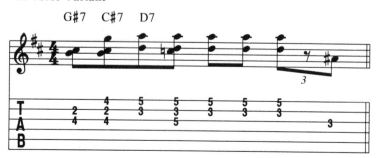

G♯7   C♯7   D7

ME AND THE DEVIL BLUES

ME AND THE DEVIL BLUES was recorded on Sunday, June 20th, 1937, in Johnson's last session. Both takes were released in the 1930s and are nearly identical. As he was with most of the other songs in his repertoire, Robert was quite sure how he wanted this one to be heard. In the lyrics, Johnson seems to be both accepting and lamenting his power-share relationship with evil, with the devil.

Satan and the imagery of the dark arts seem to have been employed as a kind of talisman or protection for itinerant bluesmen – (the same sort of role that organized crime was to play later for some other entertainers, in a much more concrete way). In their extremely public and vulnerable position – highly visible strangers in every town, often the object of women's affections – itinerant musicians needed to align themselves with an ally that might dissuade members of the local community from violence. Jealous of their talent, their apparent freedom to move about in the world, or the attention they received from the opposite sex, local men (and occasionally women) injured or murdered musicians. These performers needed the biggest, baddest heavyweight around: someone who could be present anywhere, anytime – seen or unseen. That didn't leave too many choices.

It must have seemed prudent for musicians to play on the superstitious and religious roots they had in common with their audiences, although it was lousy protection when the chips did come down. Even walking hand in hand with the Devil didn't do Robert any good on that hot August night in Greenwood, MS. Perhaps it was just a style of blues rhetoric – a conceit that many musicians frequently used, while a few must have desperately hoped it was something more.

"Me And The Devil Blues" has been recorded by John Hammond and was included in the soundtrack for the movie *Pump Up The Volume,* performed by The Cowboy Junkies. Johnny Winter also borrowed a verse from it for his recording of Johnson's "Kindhearted Woman Blues" in the late '60s.

Johnson's recording is in the key of B-flat. Robert's guitar is in standard tuning, with a capo on the 1st fret. It is transcribed in A, to preserve the original fingerings.

DAL-398-2

1. Early this mornin' – when you knocked upon my door.
   Early this mornin', oo – when you knocked upon my door.
   And I said, "Hello, Satan – I believe it's time to go.

2. Me and the Devil – was walkin' side by side.
   Me and the Devil, ooo – was walkin' side by side.
   I'm goin' to beat my woman – until I get satisfied.

3. She say you don't see why – that I will dog her 'round.
   (*spoken:* 'Now, baby, you know you ain't doin' me right, now.')
   She say you don't see why, oo – that I will dog her 'round.
   It must-a be that old evil spirit – so deep down in the ground.

4. You may bury my body – down by the highway side.
   (*spoken:* 'Baby, I don't care where you bury my body when I'm dead and gone.')
   You may bury my body, ooo – down by the highway side.
   So my old evil spirit – can get a Greyhound bus and ride.

Me And The Devil Blues

Words and Music by Robert Johnson

Capo 1st fret

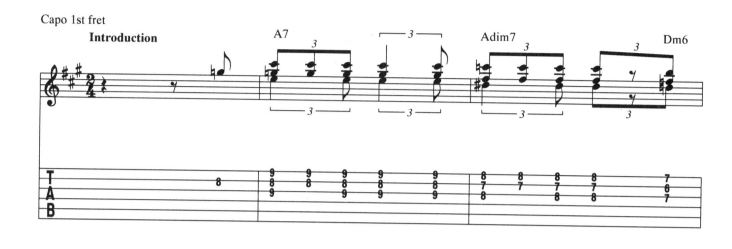

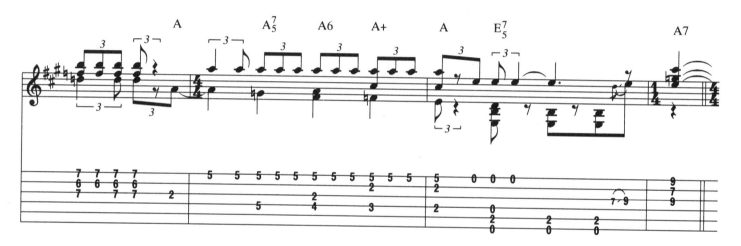

1.) Ear - ly this morn - ing ___ when you knocked up-on ___ my door,

P.M. on ⑥ and ⑤ throughout

STOP BREAKIN' DOWN

STOP BREAKIN' DOWN was originally released on the Vocalion label, with "Honeymoon Blues" on the flip side. Cocaine seems to haunt the repeated chorus lines of this tune ("...the stuff I got'll bust your brains out, baby...") and becomes explicit in the fourth verse with the use of a black idiom for the drug "...ninety-nine degree." 'Stuff' also continues to be used in black slang as a euphemism for one's sexual organs. The Rolling Stones recorded a characteristically sexy version of this tune for their **Exile On Main Street** album.

Johnson's recording is in the key of A, in open A-tuning (E-A-E-A-C♯-E). He plays it with a slide on his fourth finger to articulate the notes on the first string while barring behind the slide with his index finger. See measure 7 for the first example of this.

DAL-399-1

1. Everytime I'm walkin' – down the streets
   Some pretty mama start breakin' – down with me
   Stop breakin' down – yes, stop breakin' down.
   The stuff I got'll bust your brains out, baby –
   Hoo-ooo – it'll make you lose your mind.

2. I can't walk the streets now, con – consolate[1] my mind
   Some no-good woman she starts breakin' down –
   Stop breakin' down – ple-ease, stop breakin' down.
   The stuff I got it don' bust your brains out –
   Hoo-ooo – it'll make you lose your mind.

3. Now, you Saturday night womens – you love to ape and clown,
   You won't do nothin' but tear a good man reputation down –
   Stop breakin' down – please, stop breakin' down –
   The stuff I got'll bust your brains out, baby –
   Hoo-ooo – it'll make you lose your mind.

4. Now, I give my baby, now, the – ninety-nine degree[2]
   She jumped up and throwed a pistol down on me –
   Stop breakin' down – please, stop breakin' down –
   Stuff I got'll bust your brains out, baby –
   Hoo-hoo – it'll make you lose your mind.

5. I can't start walkin' – down the streets –
   But some pretty mama don't start breakin' down with me –
   Stop breakin' down – yes, stop breakin' down.
   The stuff I got'll bust your brains out, baby –
   Hoo-ooo-it'll make you lose your mind.

[1] **consolate:** an archaic word surviving as the root of 'console', 'consolation'.

[2] **ninety-nine degree:** According to Willie Moore, a Robinsonville musician who played with Johnson in the early '30s, this was a slang term for cocaine – which lends a literal meaning to the sexual conceit of the chorus lines ('The stuff I got'll bust your brains out, baby. It'll make you lose your mind.').

Stop Breakin' Down

Words and Music by Robert Johnson

The stuff I got 'll bust your brains out, ba-by. Hoo, — it-'ll make you lose your

mind. —

4.) Now I give —

TRAVELING RIVERSIDE BLUES

TRAVELING RIVERSIDE BLUES is the seventh of ten songs recorded in Johnson's last session, Sunday, June 20, 1937 in Dallas. Johnson recorded it in the key of B-flat, with his guitar in open A-tuning (E-A-E-A-C♯-E) and a capo on the first fret.

Some of the lyrics to this tune will be strangely familiar to fans of late 60s rock 'n' roll – the British rock group Led Zeppelin appropriated some of Johnson's lyrics for their '69 hit, "Whole Lotta Love."

The locations mentioned in the tune, Vicksburg, Friars Point, Rosedale and Tennessee (we assume, Memphis), all lie on a 230 mile stretch of the Mississippi, which was the equivalent of today's interstate for black musicians in the '30s. Of these towns, it is Friars Point which commands our attention: Johnson's highly sexual, almost self-destructive fascination with his "Friars Point rider" dominates the lyrics with a vividness practically unknown in contemporary music (and probably the reason the tune remained unissued until 1962). A fairly sleepy river town now, Friars Point was the place you came to catch the ferry or a skiff if you wanted to take a legal drink across the river in West Helena, Arkansas.

Lying in the shadow of a floodwall that actually blocks the river from view, Friars Point was abandoned as the county seat in 1930 after repeated flooding. Because of its abandonment by the white power structure and its proximity to the legal whiskey of West Helena, Friars Point became a regular stop for intinerant black musicians during the 1930s.

As notated here, the final sixteenth-note figure in the second beat of measure 11 (its first appearance) is played with the right hand thumb (A) and then index finger (G♯). It is possible, perhaps likely, that Johnson played both these notes with his thumb, picking down for the first note (A) and up with the back of the thumbnail for the second (G♯). There are passages where it actually seems to be alternately played each of these ways – sometimes there is a clear articulation of the G♯ which would be consistent with the first method, and sometimes it is less distinct which may indicate the upward brush with the back of the thumbnail. I have seen numerous traditional blues guitarists use back thumbing to establish a shuffling rhythmic bed on the low strings, and even heard bluesman John Jackson of Fairfax Station, Virginia, use alternating down and upward thumbstrokes to pick bass runs similar to flat-picking figures. It seems plausible that Johnson as well might have used this technique occasionally.

Eric Clapton borrowed the fourth verse for Cream's version of "Cross Road Blues," while John Hammond released a version of the tune on both his ***Mirrors*** and ***Best of the Country Blues*** albums.

DAL-400-2

1. If your man get personal – want to have your fun,
   If your man get personal – want to have your fun,
   Just come on back to Friars Point, mama, barrelhouse all night long.

2. I got womens in Vicksburg – clean on into Tennessee,
   I got womens in Vicksburg – clean on into Tennessee,
   But my Friars Point rider, now, hops all over me.

3. I ain't gonna state no color but her front teeth 's crowned with gold.
   Ain't gonna state no color but her front teeth 's crowned with gold.
   She's got a mortgage on my body 'n' a lien on my soul.

4. Lord, I'm goin' to Rosedale, gon' take my rider by my side,
   Lord, I'm goin' to Rosedale, gon' take my rider by my side,
   We can still barrelhouse, baby, 'cause it's on the riverside.

5. Now you can squeeze my lemon 'til the juice runs down my...
   (*spoken:* 'Til the juice run down my leg, baby, you know what I'm talkin' about.)
   You can squeeze my lemon 'til the juice run down my leg,
   (*spoken:* That's what I'm talkin' 'bout now.)
   But I'm goin' back to Friars Point, if I be rockin' to my head.[1]

[1] **rockin' to my head:** This expression has been understood variously to indicate mental incapacity, drunkeness, etc., or to be an idiomatic sexual expression of unknown origin.

Traveling Riverside Blues

Words and Music by Robert Johnson

just come on back to Friar's Point ma-ma. Bar-rel-house all night long.

2nd Verse

2.) I got wom-ens in Vicks-burg, clean on in-to Ten-nes-see.

I got wom-ens in Vicks-burg,

clean on in - to Ten - nes-see. __

But my Friar's __

N.C.
(D)

__ Point _ rid - er now, __ hops all o - ver me. __

A

3rd Verse

3.) I ain't gon - na   state no   col - or, but her   front teeth's   crowned with gold. __

Ain't gon-na   state no   col-or, but her   front teeth's   crowned with gold.

She's got a   mort-gage on _ my bod-y,'n' a

lien _ on my _ soul. _

Lord, I'm go'n' ___ to Rose-dale, gon-na take my rid-er by my side. ___

Lord, I'm go'n' ___ to Rose-dale, gon-na take my rid-er by my side.

We can still ___ bar-rel-house, ba-by, 'cause it's

by the riv-er - side. ___

HONEYMOON BLUES

was recorded in Johnson's last session (Sunday, June 20, 1937), and was released on Vocalion on the flip side of "Stop Breakin' Down Blues" (Vo 04002). Following the sexual promise of "Traveling Riverside Blues" and coming before the definitive "Love In Vain," this tune seems to draw its sentiment from the emotional middle ground between these tunes (while foreshadowing the conclusions of "Love In Vain"). It is a fairly straightforward A-blues, with a subtle suspension of the E^7_5 fragment in measures 14 and 26. Johnson was in standard tuning with a capo on the 2nd fret, and employed figures he used in other A-blues (see "Kindhearted Woman Blues" and "Me and the Devil Blues").

DAL-401-1

1. Betty Mae, Betty Mae – you shall be my wife someday.
   Betty Mae, Betty Mae – you shall be my wife someday.
   I wants a little sweet girl that will do anything that I say.

2. Betty Mae, you is my heartstring. You is my destiny.
   Betty Mae, you is my heartstring. You is my destiny.
   And you rolls across my mind, baby, each and every day.

3. Li'l girl, li'l girl – my life seem so misery.
   Hmm, – hmm-mmmm, li'l girl – my life seem so misery.
   Baby, I guess it must be love, now – Hoo-oommmm, Lord, that's takin' effect on me.

4. Someday I will return – with the marriage license in my hand.
   Someday I will return – hoo, hoo – 'th a marriage license in my hand.
   I'm 'on' take you for a honeymoon in some long, long distant land.

Honeymoon Blues

Words and Music by Robert Johnson

*See variant for last verse (meas. 20,21).

Variant for Meas. 20-21.

LOVE IN VAIN is preceded by Johnson's only unaccompanied speech ever recorded, "I wanna go on with our next one myself." The tune itself is solidly in the blues idiom, but its structure is unlike any other blues, with its persistent repetition of "All my love's in vain" at the conclusion of each verse. When the Rolling Stones covered this tune in the early '70s they left off this final line, which even in Johnson's time may have given the song an almost incantational and archaic quality. It is recorded in standard tuning, with a capo on the 2nd fret.

DAL-402-1

1. And I followed her to the station – with her suitcase in my hand.
   And I followed her to the station – with her suitcase in my hand.
   Well, it's hard to tell, it's hard to tell –
   when all your love's in vain.
   All my love's in vain.

2. When the train rolled up to the station, I looked her in the eye.
   When the train rolled up to the station and I looked her in the eye.
   Well, I was lonesome, I felt so lonesome –
   and I could not help but cry.
   All my love's in vain.

3. When the train, it left the station – with two lights on behind.
   When the train, it left the station – with two lights on behind.
   Well, the blue light was my blues – and the red light was my mind.
   All my love's in vain.

4. Ou-hoo-oo-oo-oo – Hoo, Willie Mae.
   Oh-wo-wo-wo-hey – Hoo, Willie Mae.
   Ou-oo-o-oo-oo-oo – Hee-vee – a-woe –.
   All my love's in vain.

Love In Vain

Words and Music by Robert Johnson

Capo 2nd fret

Introduction

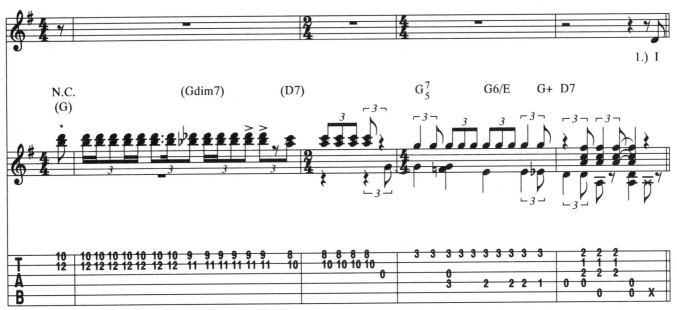

*Harmonies implied by diads (two note "chords").

Verse

fol-lowed her _____ to the sta-tion _____ with her suit-case in my hand. _____

*P.M. throughout

*Mute downstems only (bass notes).

MILKCOW'S CALF BLUES is the last piece Johnson recorded. Due to the derivative nature of its title and theme (listen to Kokomo Arnold's successful 1934 release of "Milk Cow Blues"), we might conclude that Robert had exhausted his repertoire of more original pieces. While there can be no doubt of the inspiration Johnson drew from the earlier recording by Arnold, "Milkcow's Calf Blues" is a very different song – borrowing only one line from Kokomo's piece. Recycling guitar figures he used in "Travelin' Riverside Blues"and "Stones In My Passway," Johnson gave us two strong and very similar takes of this tune.

The recording is in B-flat. Robert's guitar was in open A-tuning and capoed at the first fret. The transcription is, accordingly, in the key of A.

DAL-403-2

MILKCOW'S CALF BLUES

1. Te-(h)ell me, milk cow – what on Earth is wrong with you?
   Hoo-ooo – , milk cow – what on Earth is wrong with you?
   Now, you have a little calf, hoo-hooo
   – and your milk is turnin' blue.

2. Now, your calf is hungry – I believe he needs a suck.
   Now, your calf is hungry – I believe he needs a suck.
   But your milk is turnin' blue, hoo-ooo –
   – I believe he's outta luck.

BRIDGE: I feel like milkin' and my cow won't come.
   I feel like chu'in' it' and my milk won't turn.
   I'm cryin' please – plea – (h)ease, don't do me wrong.
   If you see my milk cow, baby now-(h)ow –
   –please–(h)ease drive her home.

3. My milk cow been ramblin', hooo – for miles around.
   My milk cow been ramblin', hoo–for miles around.
   Well, now, can you suck on some other man's bull cow –
   hoo – in this strange man's town?

Milkcow's Calf Blues

Words and Music by Robert Johnson

what on _ earth is wrong with you? _   Aw, you

have a lit-tle _ new _ calf, _ hoo, ___   and your milk is turn-in' blue. _

Verse

2.) Aw, your calf is hun-gry,   I be-lieve he needs to suck. _

I be-lieve he needs to suck. _ Now your calf is hun - gry,

hoo hoo, I be - lieve he needs to suck. _ But your

milk is turn-in' blue, _ hoo, _ I be-lieve he's out-ta luck. _

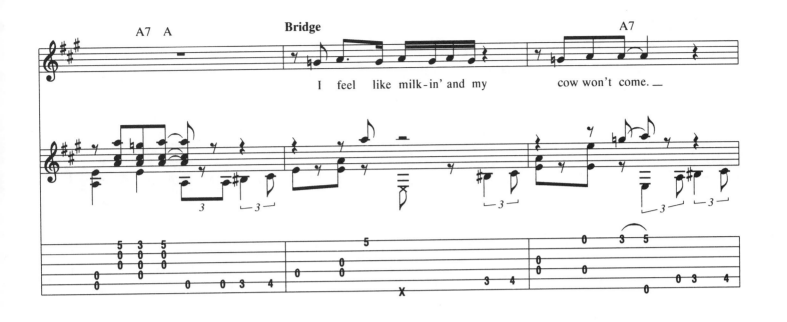

I feel like milk-in' and my cow won't come. —

I feel like chu'n-in' and my — milk won't turn. — I'm cry'n' please, —

plea - (h)ease, don't do me wrong. — If you

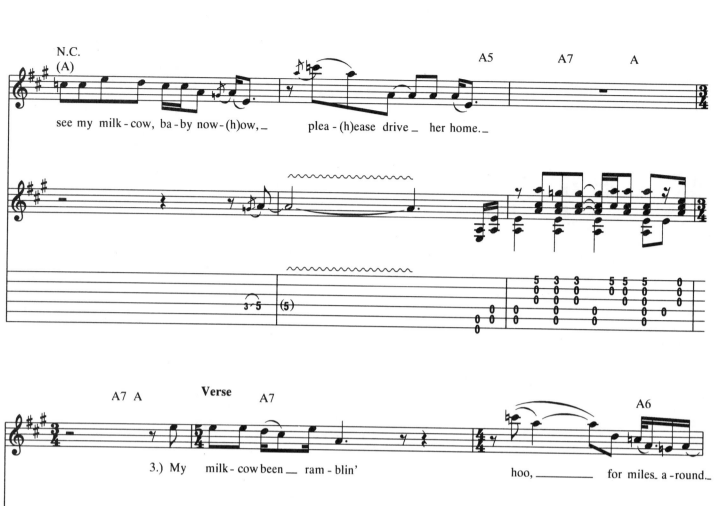

*Slap guitar body

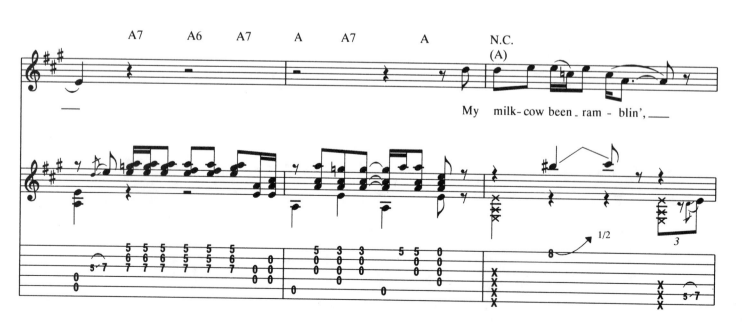

hoo, __ for miles a-round. __

Well,

now can you on suck some oth- er man's __ milk -cow, hoo, __ in this strange man's town? __

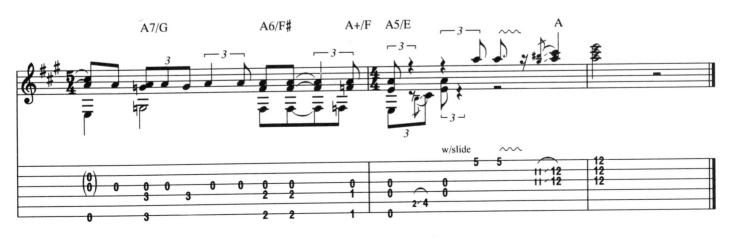

NOTATION LEGEND

126

EPILOGUE

In recent years, Robert Johnson has often been portrayed as a natural genius in a vacuum – a musician who came out of nowhere cutting a wide swath across the Delta as he seemed to be propelled toward an early grave. As appealing as this may be to dream about, finally it is just a dream. Johnson was a singular musician of extraordinary talent, but he came out of somewhere. And he had good company. Robert Johnson is survived by a number of his contemporaries who continue to create and perform music with similar style and passion. Below you will find the senior musicians who helped with this project. These are men who lived that life and made that music and who are still here with us today actively pursuing their careers.

David 'Honeyboy' Edwards lives in Chicago and may be contacted for bookings in care of Michael Frank, 1818 Pratt Boulevard, Chicago, IL 60629. He has recorded a number of fine albums:

> *Blues, Blues, Blues* (Roots LPS 518, Austria)
> *I've Been Around* (Trix LPS 3319)
> *Mississippi Delta Blues Man* (Folkways LPS 3539)
> *Walking Blues* (Flyright LPS 541, England)
> *Old Friend* (Earwig 4902)
> *White Windows* (Blue Suit BS102)

Robert Lockwood, Jr. lives in Cleveland, Ohio where he has a blues festival every July 4th. For more information about the festival or bookings contact Mr. Lockwood at 7203 Lawnview Avenue, Cleveland, OH 44103. He has a number of excellent albums including:

> *Steady Rolling Man* (Delmark 630)
> *The Baddest New Guitar* (P-Vine 2134, Japan)
> *What's the Score* (P-Vine 2290)

Johnny Shines currently lives in Tuscaloosa, Alabama. He may be reached for bookings by writing Johnny & Candy Martin Shines, P.O. Box 1962, Tuscaloosa, AL 35403. Mr. Shines has many exciting recordings available, as well, including:

> *Nobody's Fault But Mine* (Black & Blue #33.541, France)
> *Hey, Ba-Ba-Re-Bop* (Rounder 2020)
> *Standing At The Crossroads* (Testament 2221)
> *Recorded Live* (Wolf LP 120.914)
> *Mr. Blues Is Here To Stay* (Rounder 2026)
> *Back To The Country* (Blind Pig 74391)

In addition to their recordings listed above, Mr. Shines and Mr. Lockwood have recorded at least two albums together:

> *Robert 'Jr.' Lockwood & Johnny Shines* (Rounder 2023)
> *Johnny Shines & Robert Lockwood, Jr.* (Flyright CD 10)

SCOTT AINSLIE

Based in Durham, North Carolina, blues guitarist
and teacher Scott Ainslie performs the acoustic
blues of Robert Johnson, Reverend Gary Davis,
Blind Blake and others on vintage, metal-bodied
National guitars and has done extensive fieldwork
with black traditional blues and gospel guitarists in
North Carolina. He has performed in Europe and
throughout the eastern United States and presented
programs as an Artist-in-Education at numerous
colleges and schools including: Queens College in
Belfast, N.I., Trinity College in Dublin, North
Carolina State University, Wesleyan College,
Columbus College and the University of South
Carolina at Lancaster. He maintains an active
schedule of teaching and performing and looks
forward to the release of his first blues recordings.